Lizzie McGuire

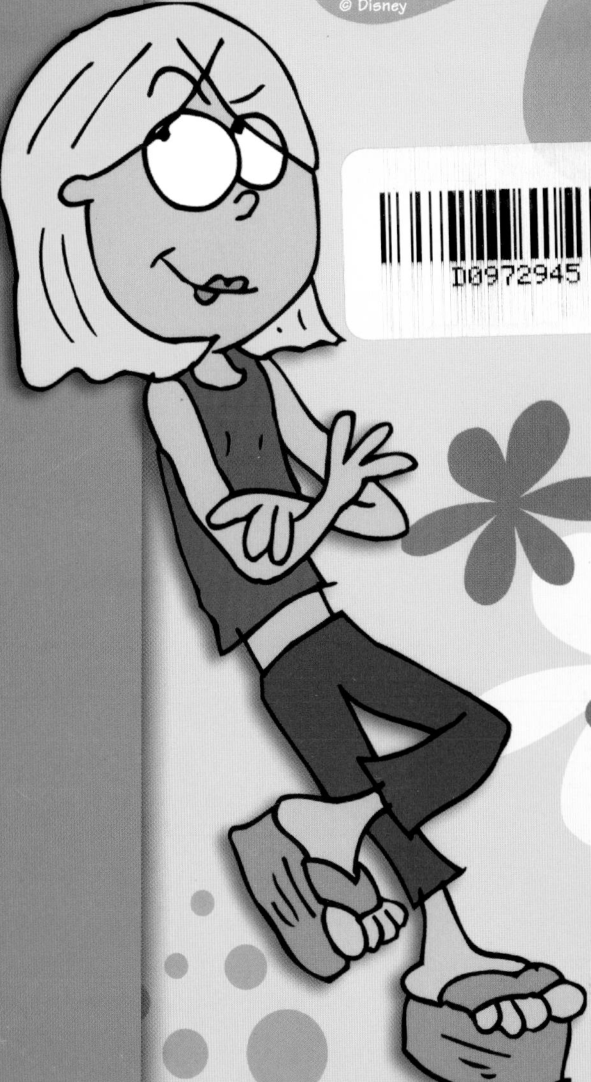

ALSO AVAILABLE FROM  TOKYOPOP®

MANGA

ANGELIC LAYER*
BABY BIRTH* (September 2003)
BRAIN POWERED* (June 2003)
BRIGADOON* (August 2003)
CARDCAPTOR SAKURA
CARDCAPTOR SAKURA: MASTER OF THE CLOW*
CHRONICLES OF THE CURSED SWORD
CLAMP SCHOOL DETECTIVES*
CLOVER
CORRECTOR YUI
COWBOY BEBOP*
COWBOY BEBOP: SHOOTING STAR* (June 2003)
DEMON DIARY
DIGIMON*
DRAGON HUNTER (June 2003)
DRAGON KNIGHTS*
DUKLYON: CLAMP SCHOOL DEFENDERS*
ESCAFLOWNE (July 2003)
FLCL* (September 2003)
FORBIDDEN DANCE* (August 2003)
GATE KEEPERS*
G-GUNDAM* (June 2003)
GRAVITATION* (June 2003)
GUNDAM WING*
GUNDAM WING: BATTLEFIELD OF PACIFISTS*
GUNDAM WING: ENDLESS WALTZ*
GUNDAM WING: THE LAST OUTPOST*
HARLEM BEAT
I.N.V.U.
INITIAL D*
JING: KING OF BANDITS* (June 2003)
JULINE
KARE KANO*
KINDAICHI CASE FILES, THE* (June 2003)
KING OF HELL (June 2003)
KODOCHA: SANA'S STAGE*
MAGIC KNIGHT RAYEARTH* (August 2003)

MAGIC KNIGHT RAYEARTH II* (COMING SOON)
MAN OF MANY FACES*
MARMALADE BOY*
MARS*
MIRACLE GIRLS
MONSTERS, INC.
NIEA_7* (August 2003)
PEACH GIRL
PEACH GIRL: CHANGE OF HEART*
PET SHOP OF HORRORS* (June 2003)
PLANET LADDER*
PLANETES* (October 2003)
RAGNAROK
RAVE MASTER*
REALITY CHECK
REBIRTH
REBOUND*
RISING STARS OF MANGA
SAILOR MOON
SAINT TAIL
SAMURAI GIRL: REAL BOUT HIGH SCHOOL*
SHAOLIN SISTERS*
SHIRAHIME-SYO: SNOW GODDESS TALES* (Dec. 2003)
THE SKULL MAN*
TOKYO MEW MEW*
VAMPIRE GAME (June 2003)
WISH*
WORLD OF HARTZ (August 2003)
ZODIAC P.I.* (July 2003)

*INDICATES 100% AUTHENTIC MANGA (RIGHT-TO-LEFT FORMAT)

CINE-MANGA™

CARDCAPTORS
JIMMY NEUTRON (September 2003)
KIM POSSIBLE
LIZZIE MCGUIRE
POWER RANGERS: NINJA STORM (August 2003)
SPONGEBOB SQUAREPANTS (September 2003)
SPY KIDS 2

NOVELS

KARMA CLUB (July 2003)
SAILOR MOON

TOKYOPOP KIDS

STRAY SHEEP (September 2003)

ART BOOKS

CARDCAPTOR SAKURA*
MAGIC KNIGHT RAYEARTH*

ANIME GUIDES

COWBOY BEBOP ANIME GUIDES
GUNDAM TECHNICAL MANUALS
SAILOR MOON SCOUT GUIDES

Lizzie McGuire

Volume 1

Series created by Terri Minsky

"Pool Party"

written by Terri Minsky

"Picture Day"

written by Douglas Tuber & Tim Maile

TOKYO • LONDON • LOS ANGELES • NEW YORK

Contributing Editor - Jodi Bryson
Graphic Design & Lettering - Yolanda Petriz
Production Specialist - Monalisa de Asis
Additional Layout - Raymond Makowski
Cover Layout - Patrick Hook

Senior Editor - Amy Court Kaemon
Managing Editor - Jill Freshney
Production Manager - Jennifer Miller
Art Director - Matt Alford
Editorial Director - Jeremy Ross
VP of Production & Manufacturing - Ron Klamert
President & C.O.O. - John Parker
C.E.O. & Publisher - Stuart Levy

Email: editor@TOKYOPOP.com
Come visit us online at www.TOKYOPOP.com

A **TOKYOPOP**® Cine-Manga™
TOKYOPOP® is an imprint of Mixx Entertainment, Inc.
5900 Wilshire Blvd., Suite 2000, Los Angeles, CA 90036

ISBN: 1-59182-147-9

First TOKYOPOP® printing: May 2003

10 9 8 7 6 5 4 3 2 1
Printed in Canada

Lizzie McGUiRE

Volume 1

CONTENTS

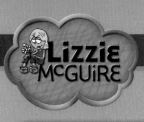

Lizzie McGuire

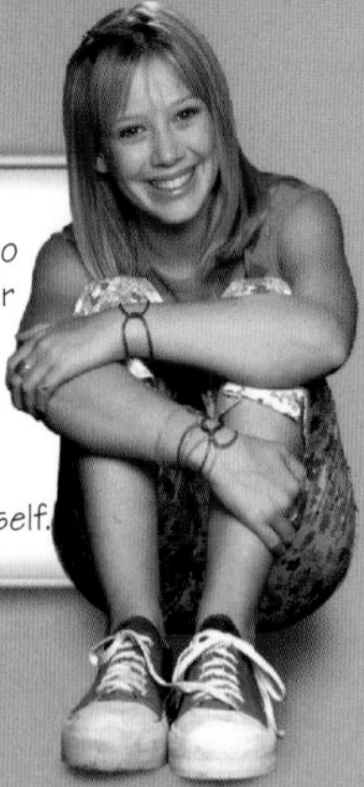

LIZZIE
A typical 14-year-old girl who has her fair share of bad hair days and embarrassing moments. Luckily, Lizzie knows how to admit when she's wrong, back up her friends, and stand up for herself.

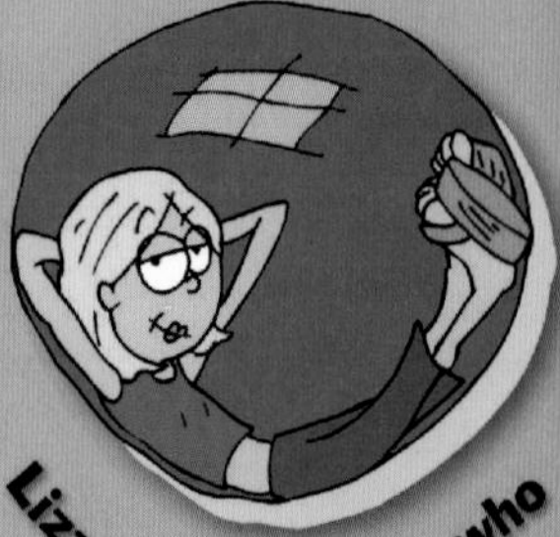

Lizzie's alter-ego, who says and does all the thin Lizzie's afraid to.

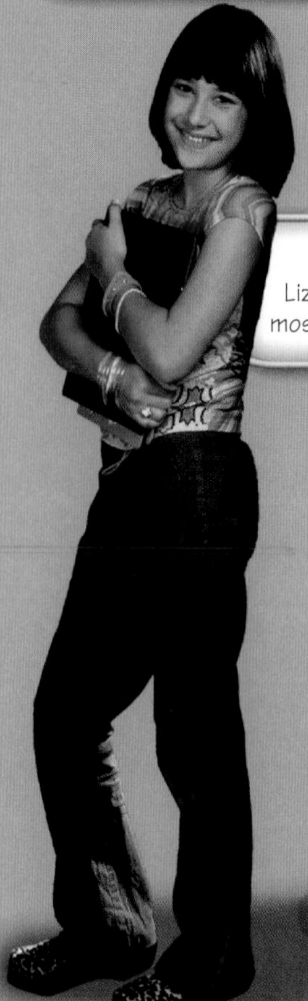

MIRANDA
Lizzie's best friend and most trusted confidante.

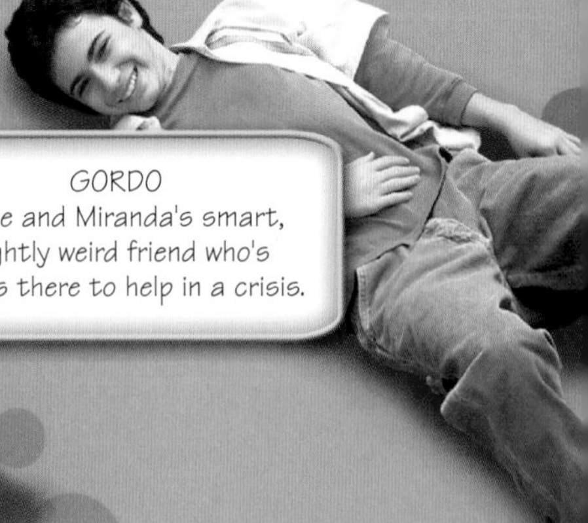

GORDO
Lizzie and Miranda's smart, slightly weird friend who's always there to help in a crisis.

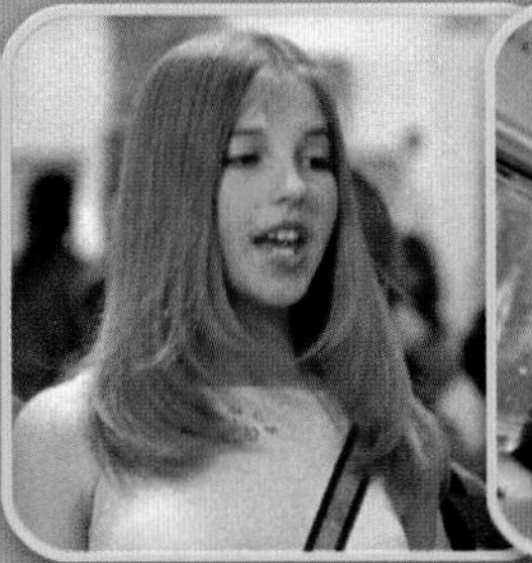

KATE
Lizzie and Miranda's ex-friend who thinks she's too good for them now that she wears a bra.

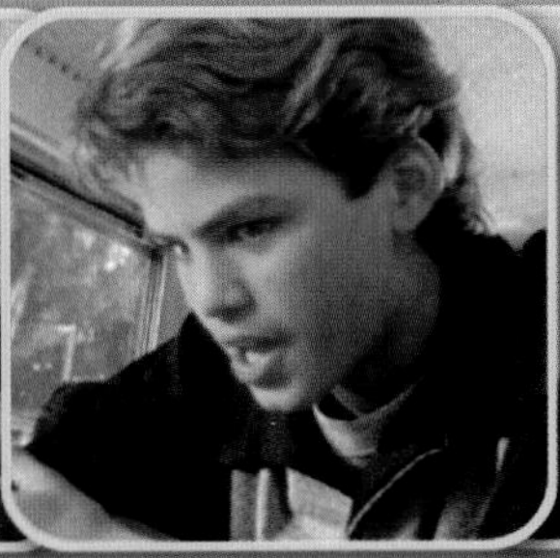

DANNY
The guy every girl in school wants as a boyfriend.

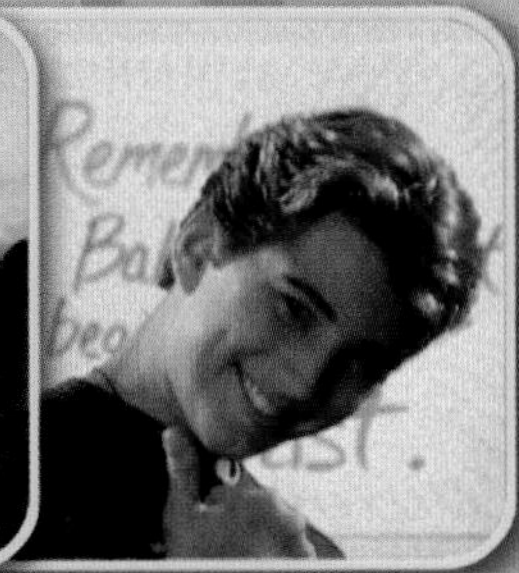

ETHAN
The most popular guy in school.

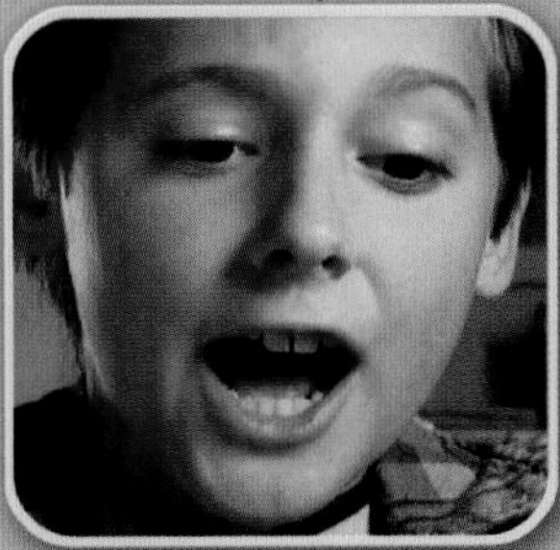

MATT
Lizzie's little brother, who spends most of his time making her crazy.

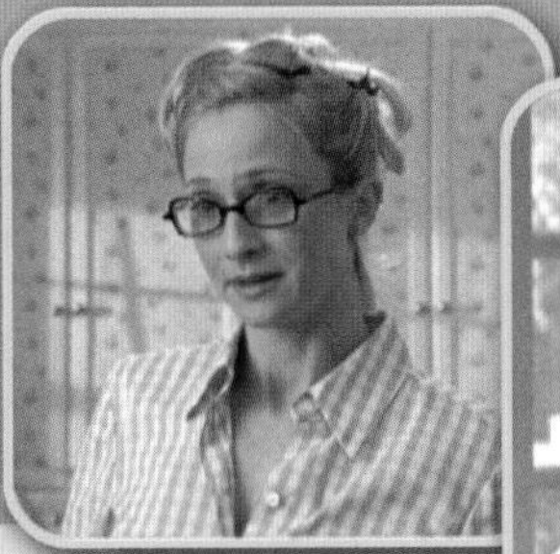

LIZZIE'S MOM, JO
She only wants the best for Lizzie, but sometimes she tries a little too hard.

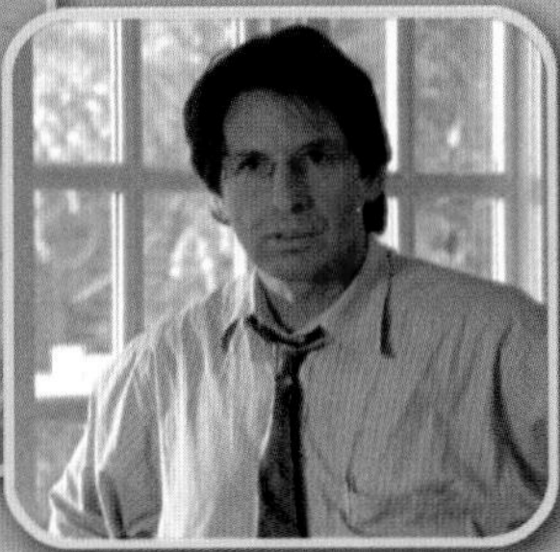

LIZZIE'S DAD, SAM
He loves Lizzie, though he doesn't always know how to relate to her.

Lizzie McGuire

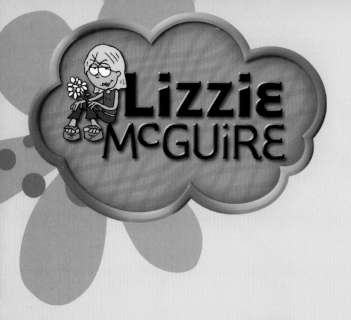

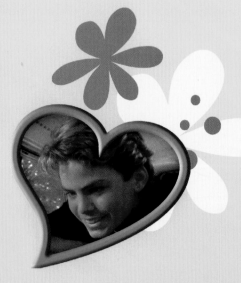

Episode 1

"Pool Party"

Lizzie and Miranda are totally psyched for Danny Kessler's pool party — until Lizzie finds out she has to go to her grandma's birthday party instead.

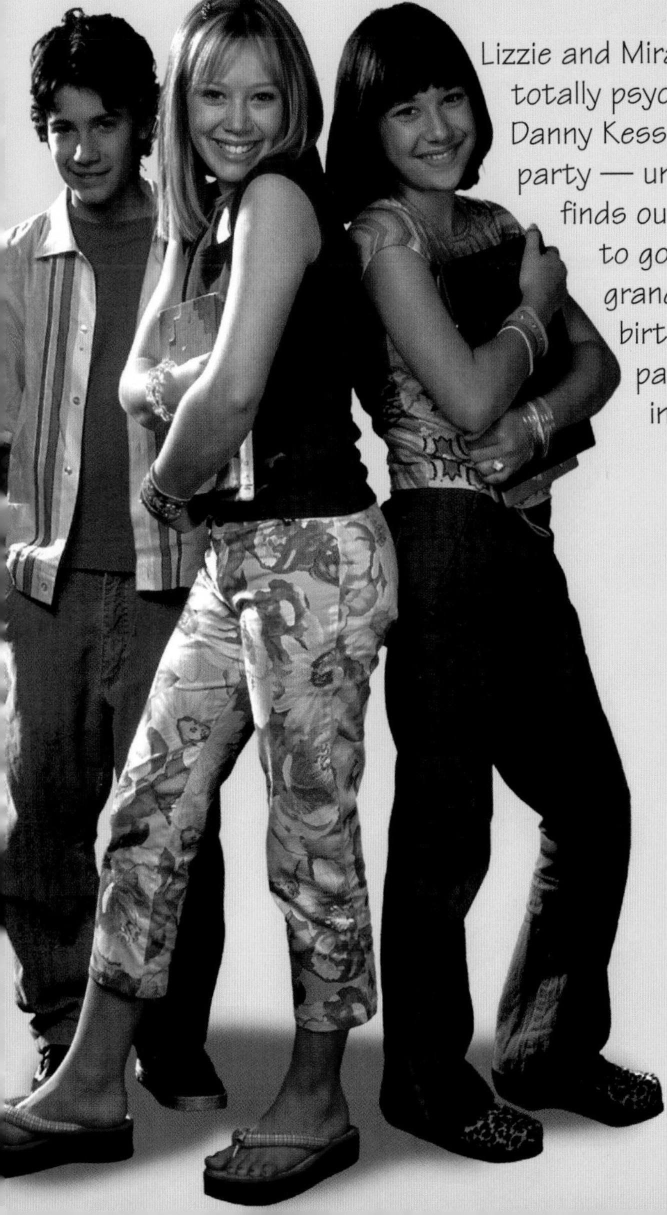

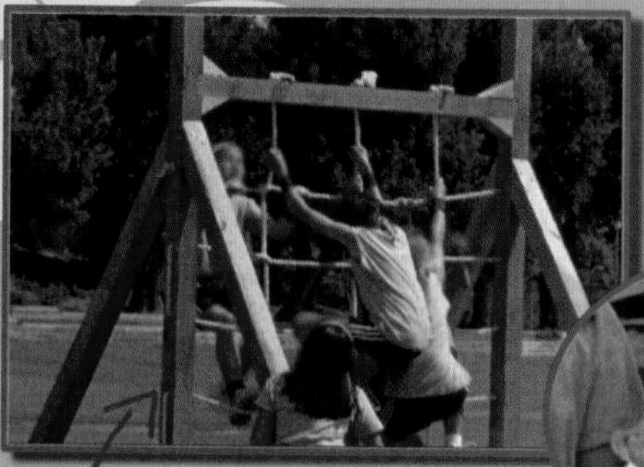

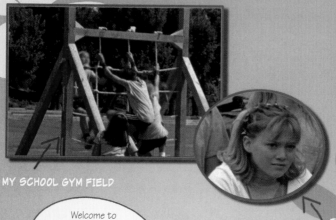

MY SCHOOL GYM FIELD

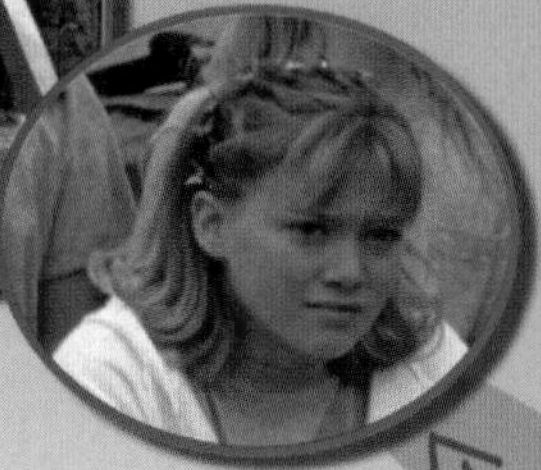

THAT'S ME IN GYM

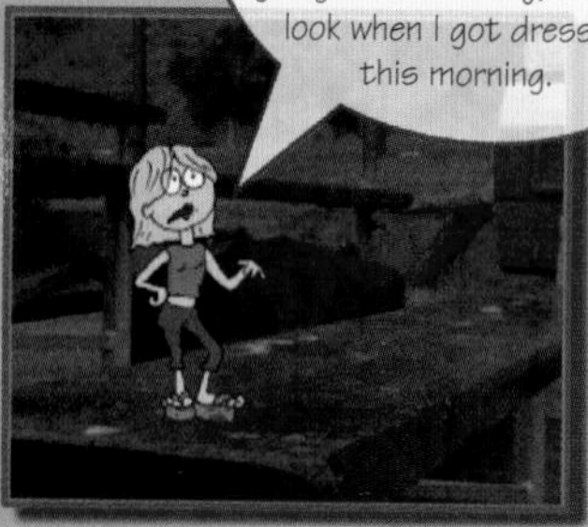
Welcome to my nightmare. Third period gym. Like, hello, I wasn't going for the sticky, sweaty look when I got dressed this morning.

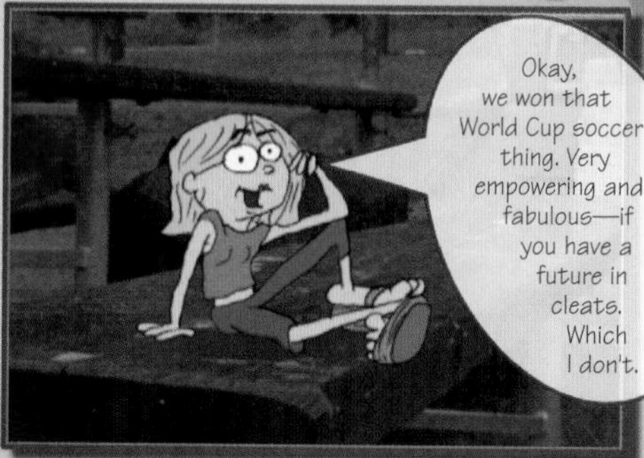
Okay, we won that World Cup soccer thing. Very empowering and fabulous—if you have a future in cleats. Which I don't.

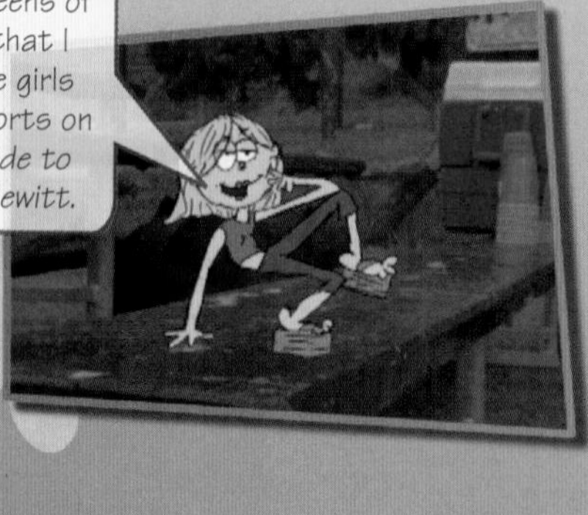
And I wouldn't exactly qualify as one of the Future Prom Queens of America. Not that I mind. These are girls who do book reports on *The Pocket Guide to Jennifer Love Hewitt.*

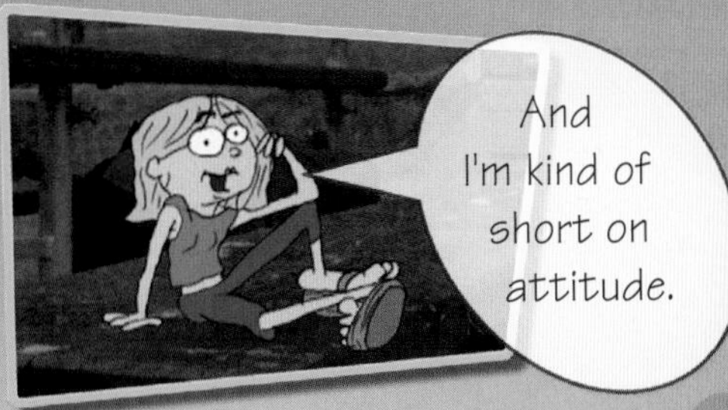
And I'm kind of short on attitude.

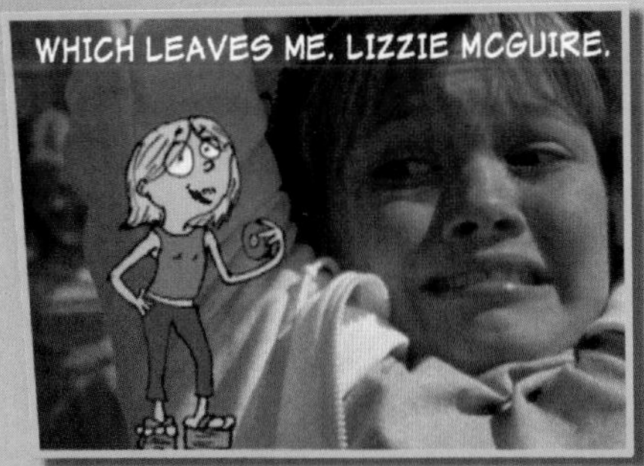
WHICH LEAVES ME. LIZZIE MCGUIRE.

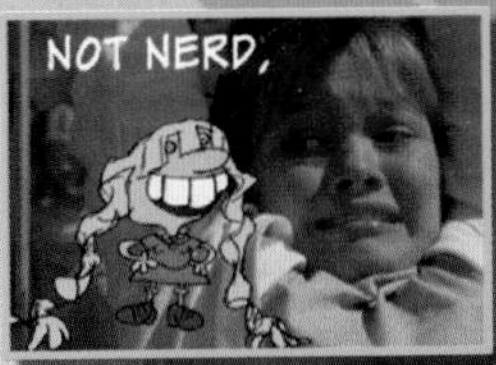
NOT NERD,

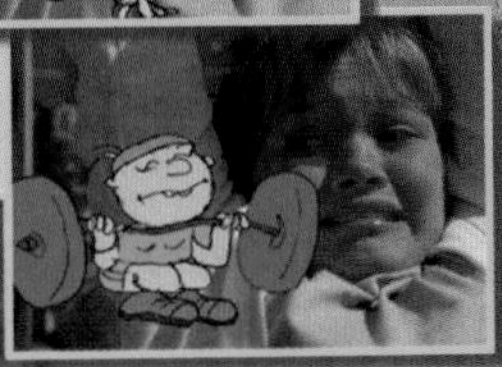

NOT JOCK,

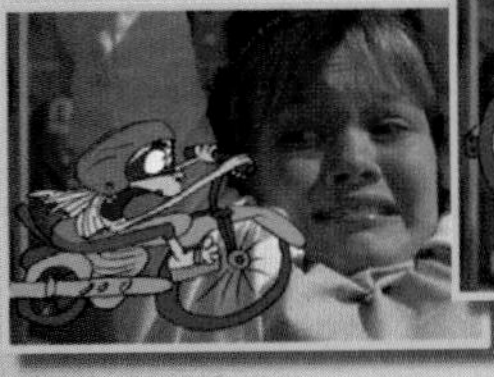

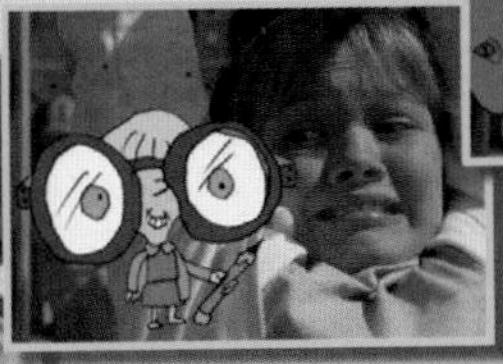

NOT BRAIN,

NOT REBEL,
NOT DIVA. I GUESS
YOU'D SAY I WAS D. AS IN:
NONE OF THE ABOVE.

ACCORDING TO MY MOM, I'M AT A VERY DIFFICULT POINT IN MY LIFE. SHE USES THE WORD "HORMONES." A LOT. MY MOM SAYS SHE REMEMBERS WHAT IT WAS LIKE WHEN SHE WAS MY AGE. SHE SAYS EVERYBODY'S GOING THROUGH THE SAME PHYSICAL AND PSYCHOLOGICAL CHANGES AS I AM — THAT WE ALL JUST HANDLE THEM DIFFERENTLY. AND EXCEPT FOR CHAT ROOMS AND BRAIN SURGEON BARBIES, THINGS AREN'T ALL THAT DIFFERENT. THAT'S WHAT MAKES US WHO WE ARE. I KNOW SHE'S TRYING TO HELP, SO I TELL HER SHE IS, BECAUSE THAT'S PRETTY MUCH THE ONLY WAY I CAN GET HER OUT OF MY ROOM.

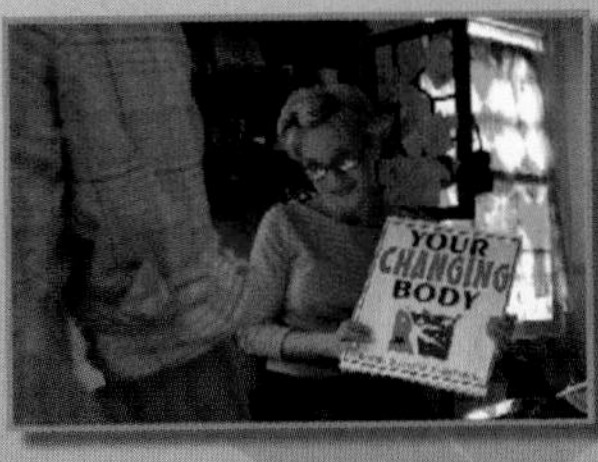
YOUR CHANGING BODY

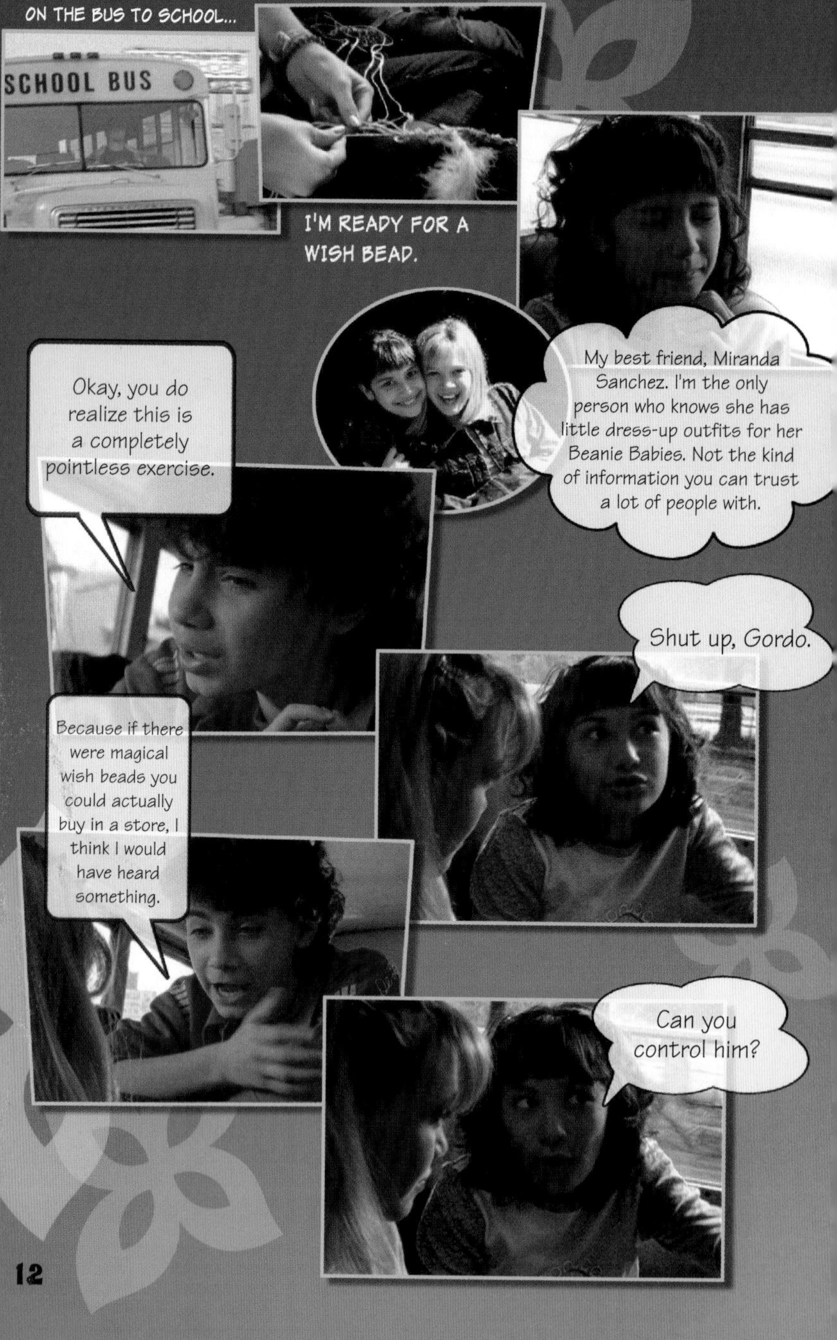
ON THE BUS TO SCHOOL...
SCHOOL BUS
I'M READY FOR A WISH BEAD.
Okay, you do realize this is a completely pointless exercise.
My best friend, Miranda Sanchez. I'm the only person who knows she has little dress-up outfits for her Beanie Babies. Not the kind of information you can trust a lot of people with.
Because if there were magical wish beads you could actually buy in a store, I think I would have heard something.
Shut up, Gordo.
Can you control him?

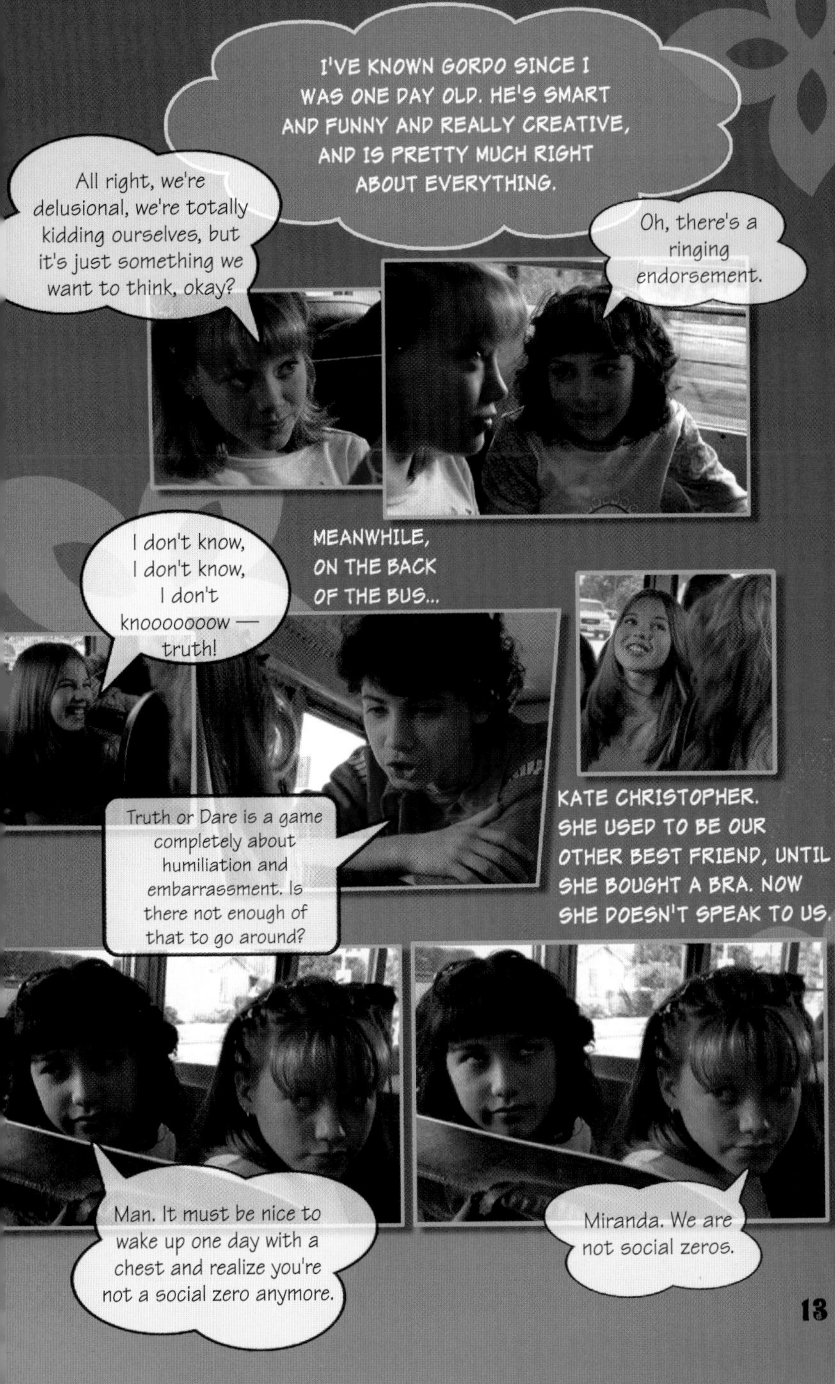

I'VE KNOWN GORDO SINCE I WAS ONE DAY OLD. HE'S SMART AND FUNNY AND REALLY CREATIVE, AND IS PRETTY MUCH RIGHT ABOUT EVERYTHING.
All right, we're delusional, we're totally kidding ourselves, but it's just something we want to think, okay?
Oh, there's a ringing endorsement.
MEANWHILE, ON THE BACK OF THE BUS...
I don't know, I don't know, I don't knoooooooow — truth!
Truth or Dare is a game completely about humiliation and embarrassment. Is there not enough of that to go around?
KATE CHRISTOPHER. SHE USED TO BE OUR OTHER BEST FRIEND, UNTIL SHE BOUGHT A BRA. NOW SHE DOESN'T SPEAK TO US.
Man. It must be nice to wake up one day with a chest and realize you're not a social zero anymore.
Miranda. We are not social zeros.

AFTER GORDO LEAVES...

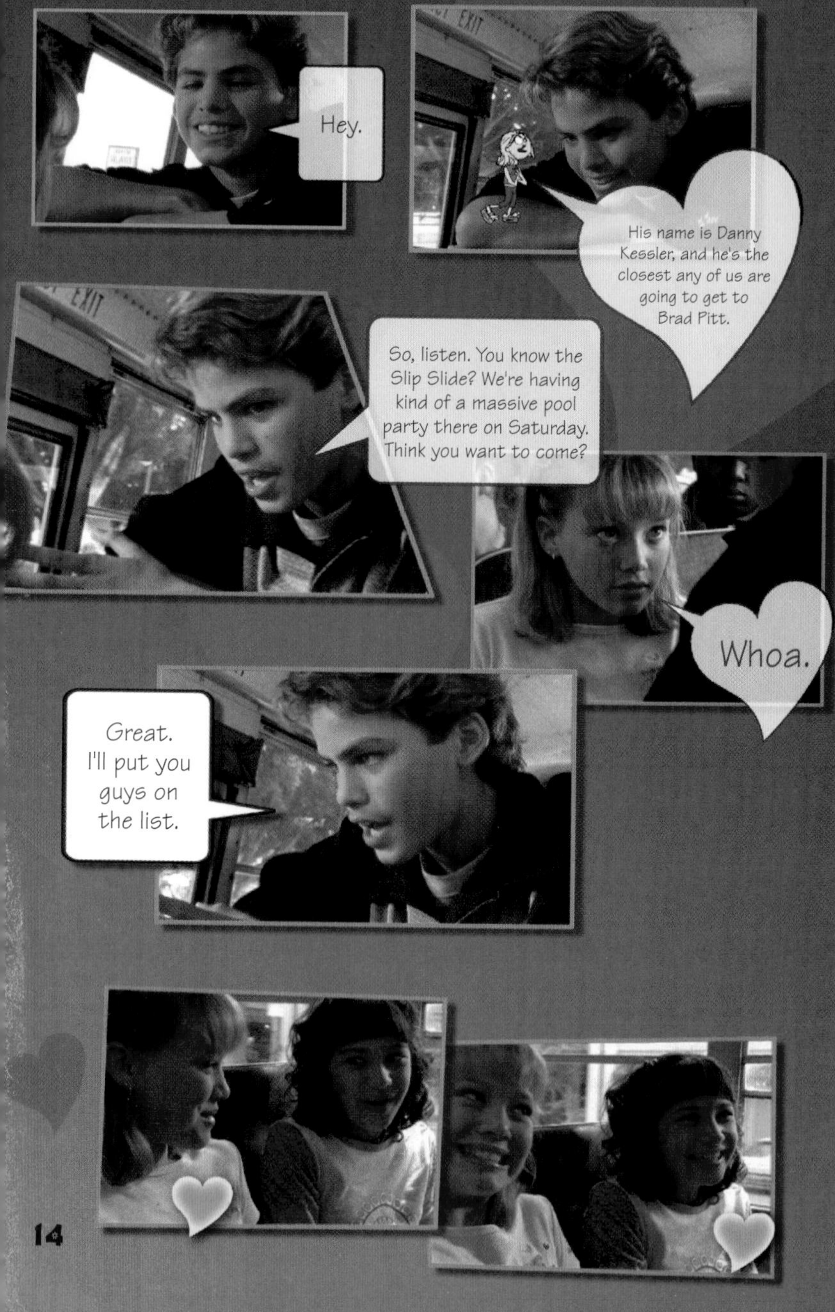
Hey.
His name is Danny Kessler, and he's the closest any of us are going to get to Brad Pitt.
So, listen. You know the Slip Slide? We're having kind of a massive pool party there on Saturday. Think you want to come?
Whoa.
Great. I'll put you guys on the list.

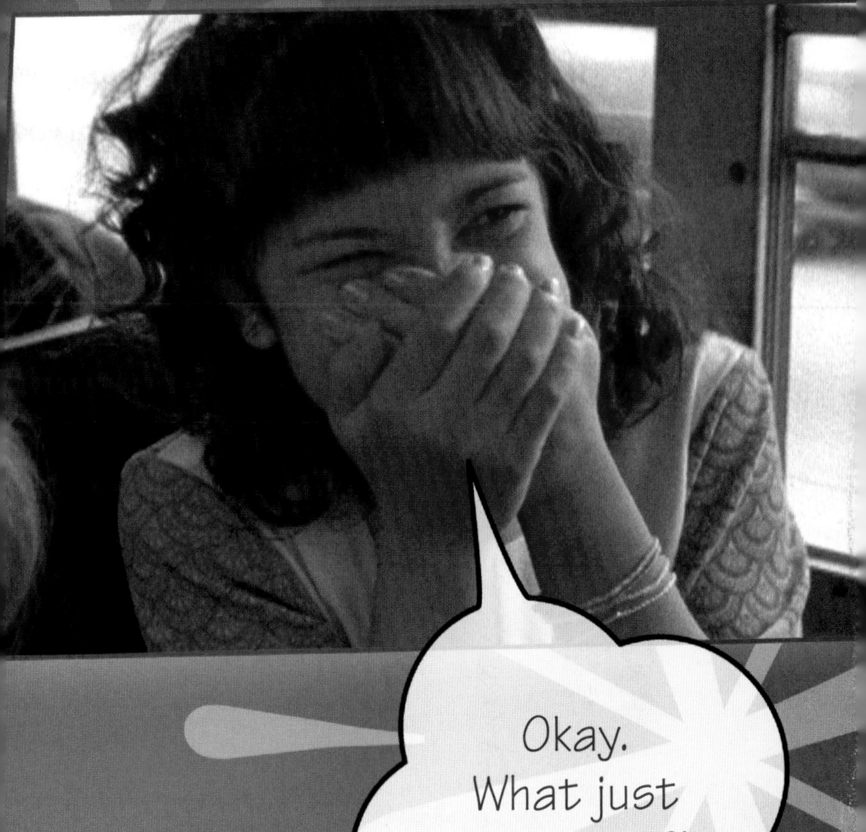

Okay.
What just
happened?!

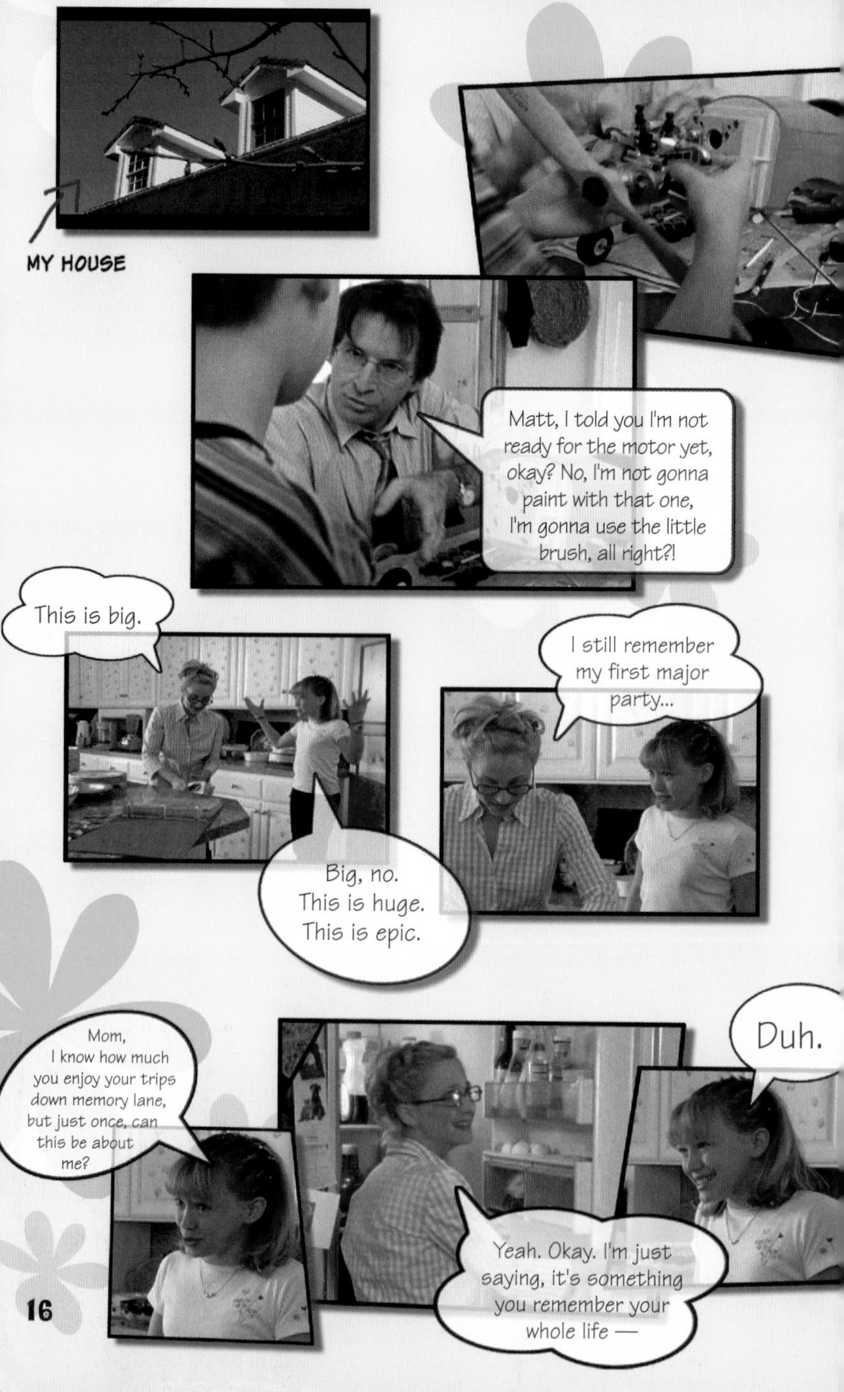
MY HOUSE
Matt, I told you I'm not ready for the motor yet, okay? No, I'm not gonna paint with that one, I'm gonna use the little brush, all right?!
This is big.
Big, no. This is huge. This is epic.
I still remember my first major party...
Mom, I know how much you enjoy your trips down memory lane, but just once, can this be about me?
Yeah. Okay. I'm just saying, it's something you remember your whole life —
Duh.

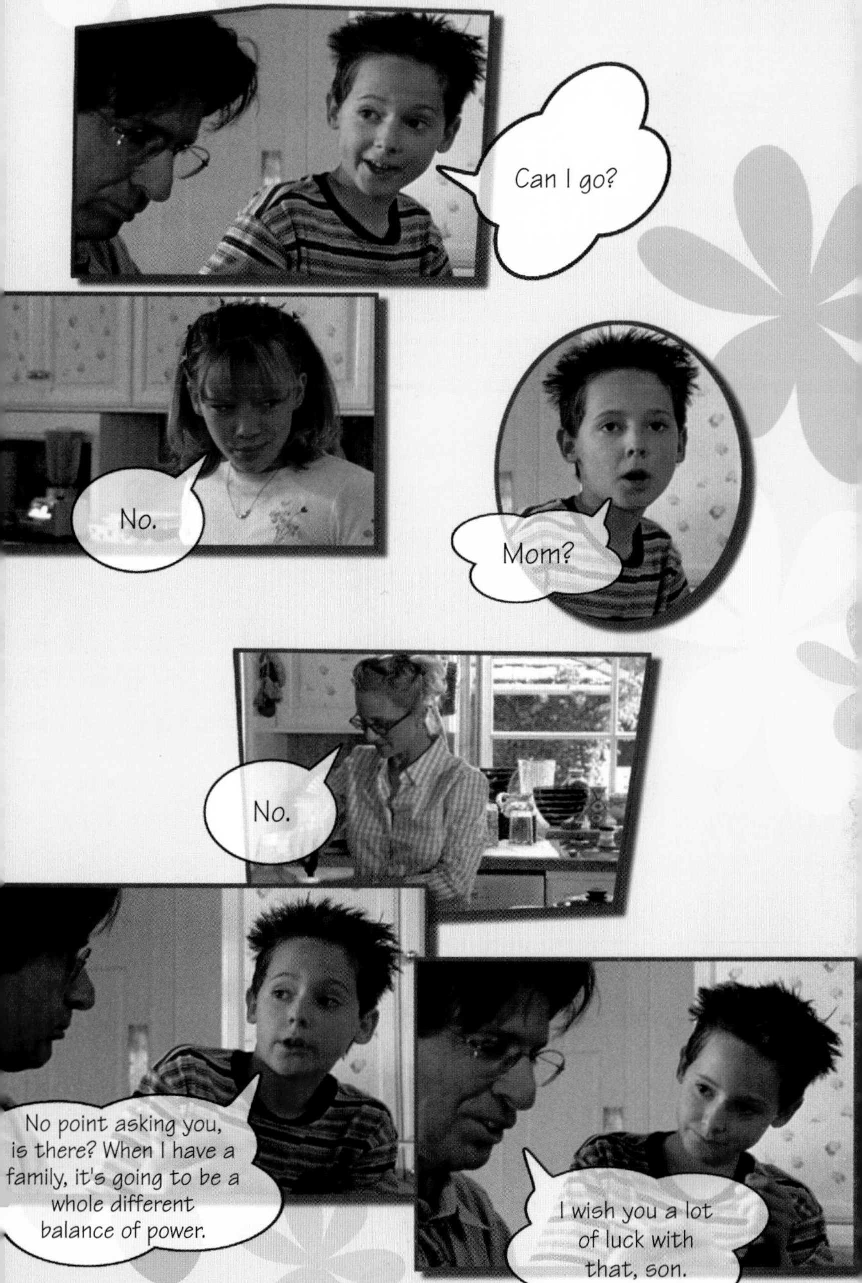
Can I go?
No.
Mom?
No.
No point asking you, is there? When I have a family, it's going to be a whole different balance of power.
I wish you a lot of luck with that, son.

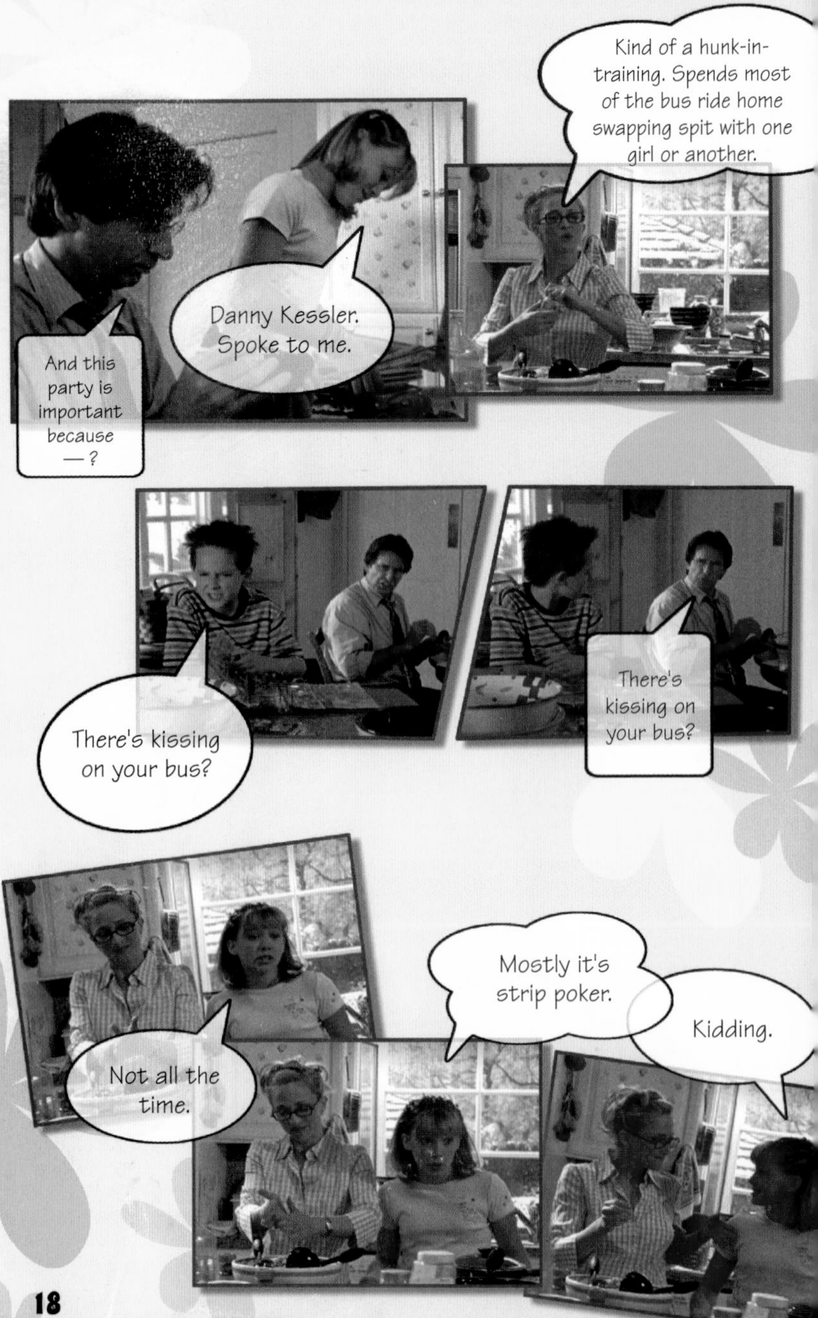
And this party is important because —?
Danny Kessler. Spoke to me.
Kind of a hunk-in-training. Spends most of the bus ride home swapping spit with one girl or another.
There's kissing on your bus?
There's kissing on your bus?
Not all the time.
Mostly it's strip poker.
Kidding.

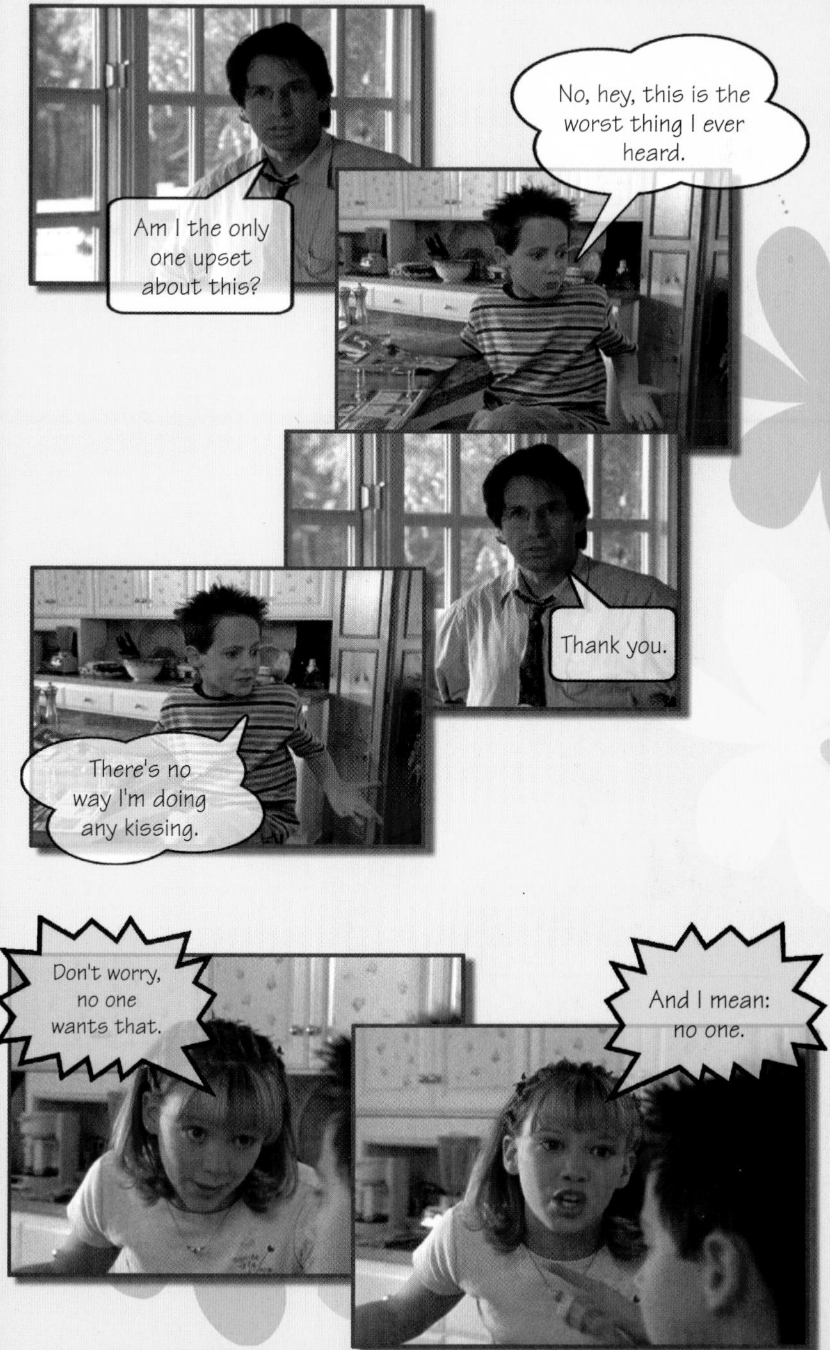
Am I the only one upset about this?
No, hey, this is the worst thing I ever heard.
Thank you.
There's no way I'm doing any kissing.
Don't worry, no one wants that.
And I mean: no one.

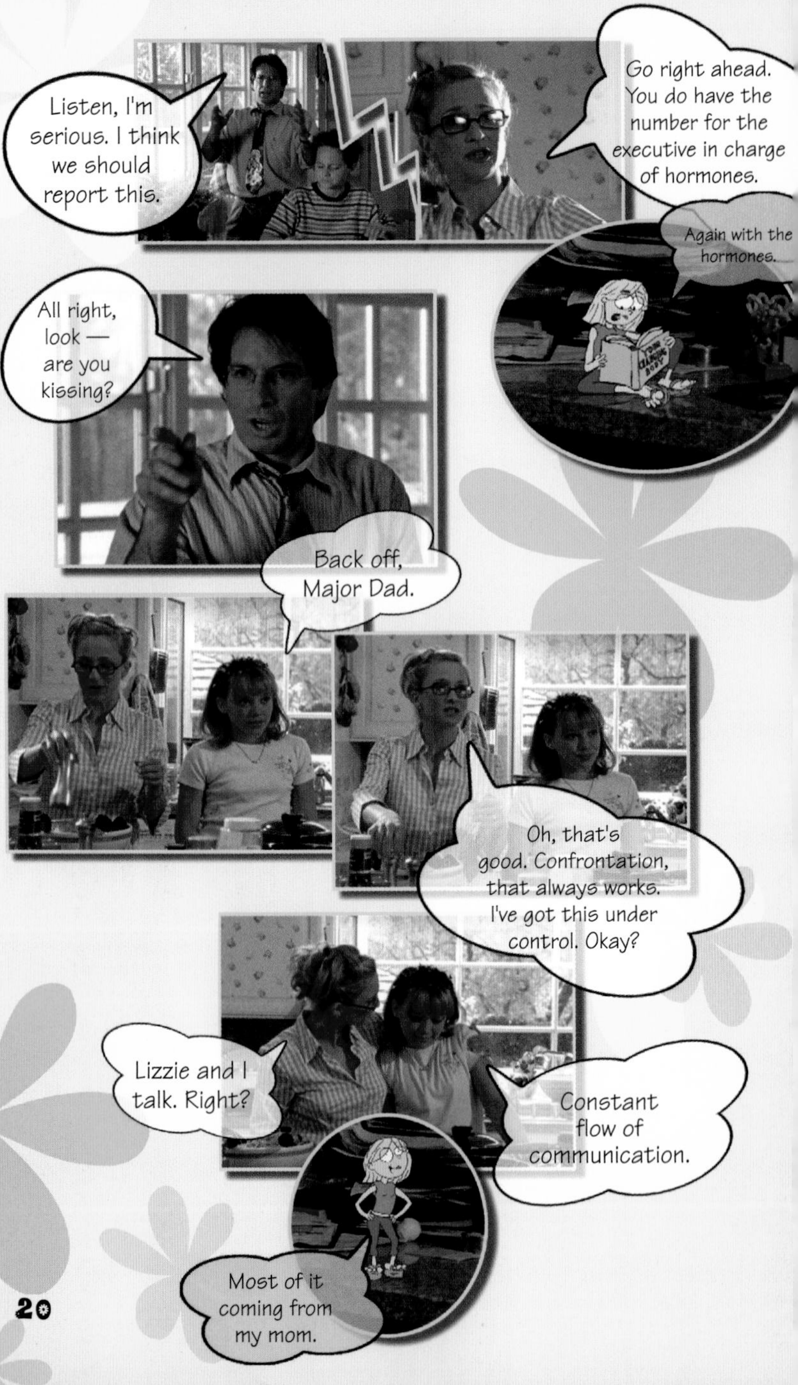

Listen, I'm serious. I think we should report this.
Go right ahead. You do have the number for the executive in charge of hormones.
Again with the hormones.
All right, look — are you kissing?
Back off, Major Dad.
Oh, that's good. Confrontation, that always works. I've got this under control. Okay?
Lizzie and I talk. Right?
Constant flow of communication.
Most of it coming from my mom.

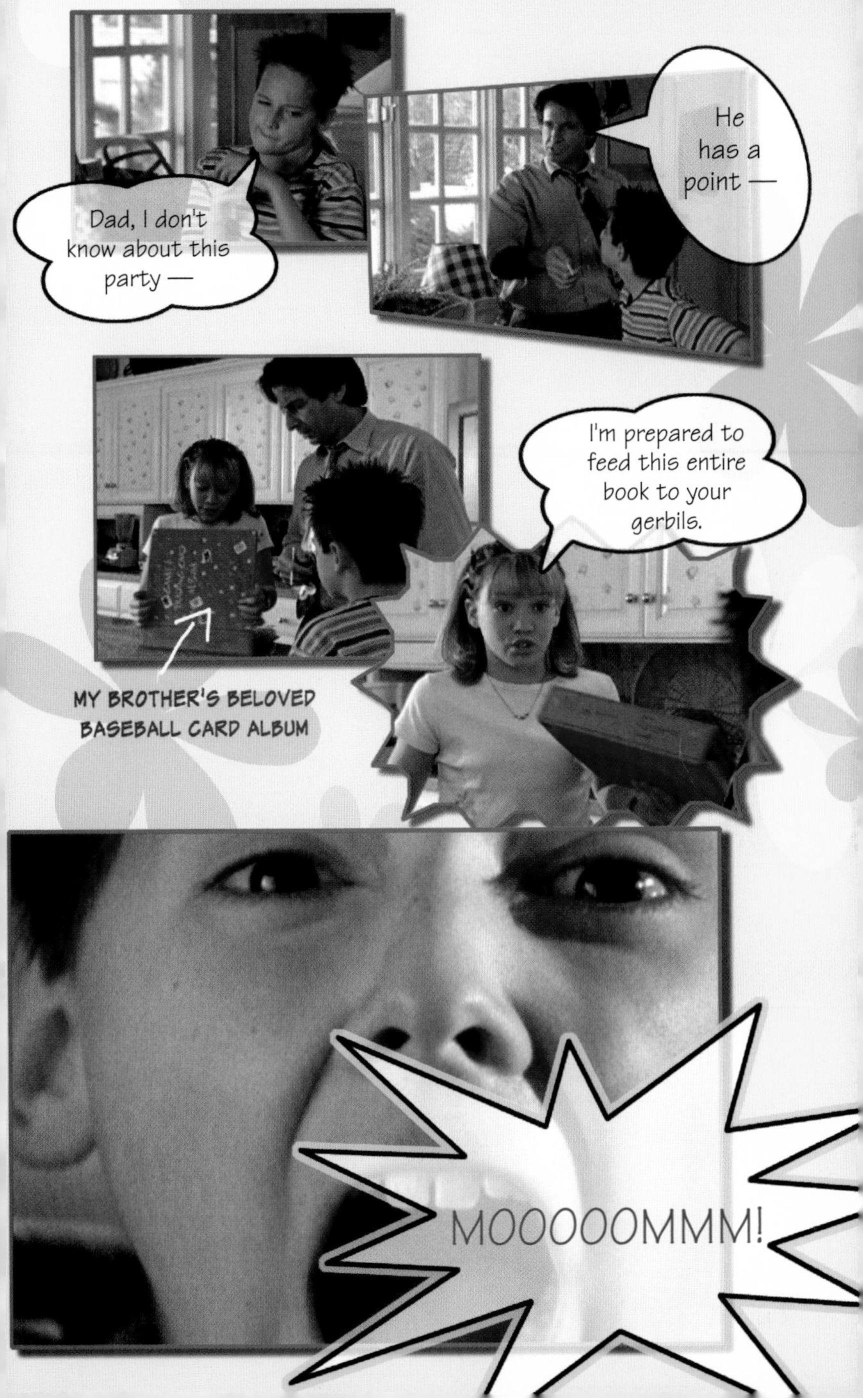
Dad, I don't know about this party —
He has a point —
I'm prepared to feed this entire book to your gerbils.
MY BROTHER'S BELOVED BASEBALL CARD ALBUM
MOOOOOMMM!

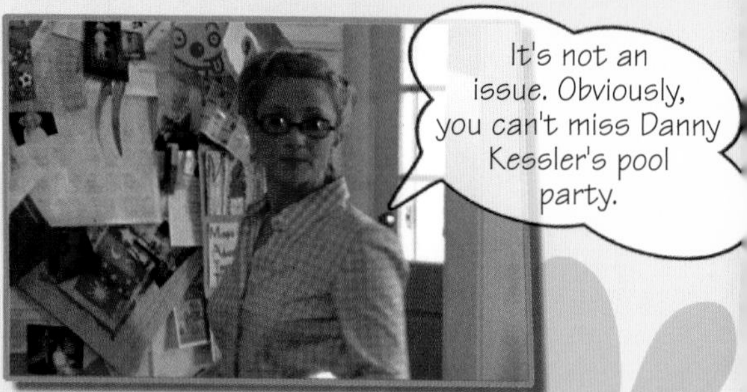
It's not an issue. Obviously, you can't miss Danny Kessler's pool party.

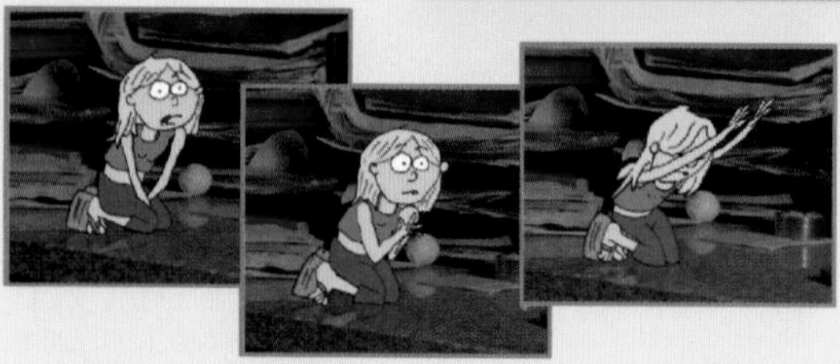

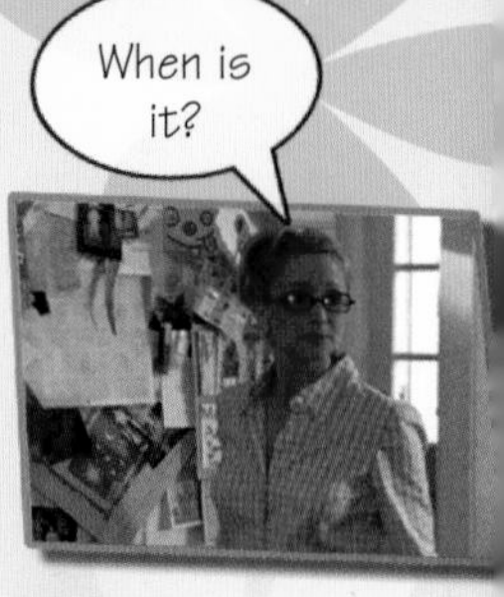
When is it?

SHE'S BEING SO GREAT. MAYBE I DON'T GIVE HER ENOUGH CREDIT.

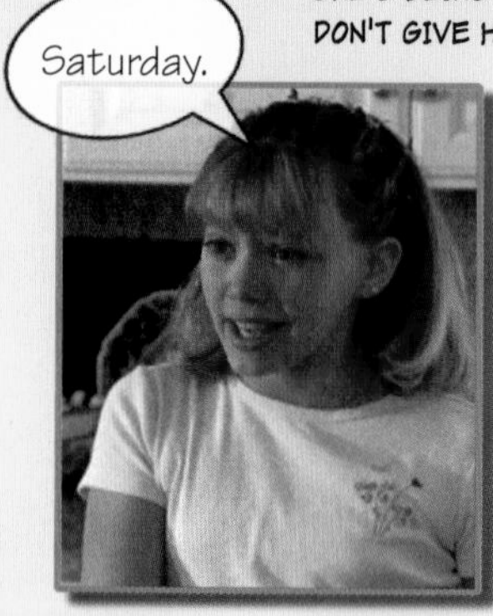
Saturday.

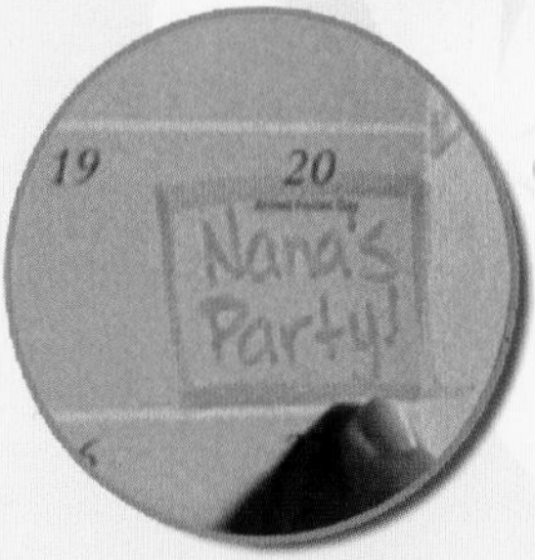
19
20
Nana's Party!

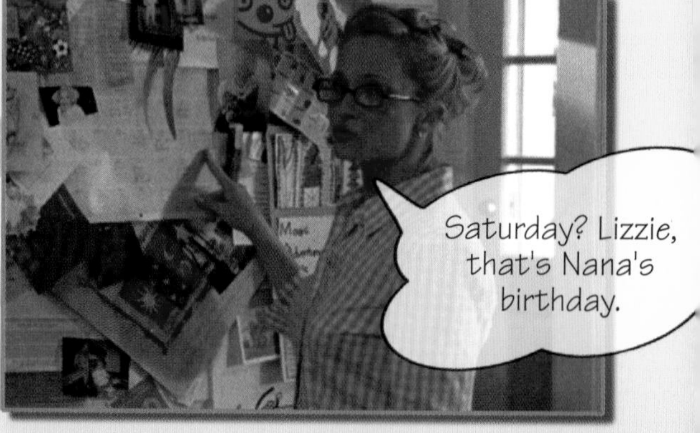
Saturday? Lizzie, that's Nana's birthday.

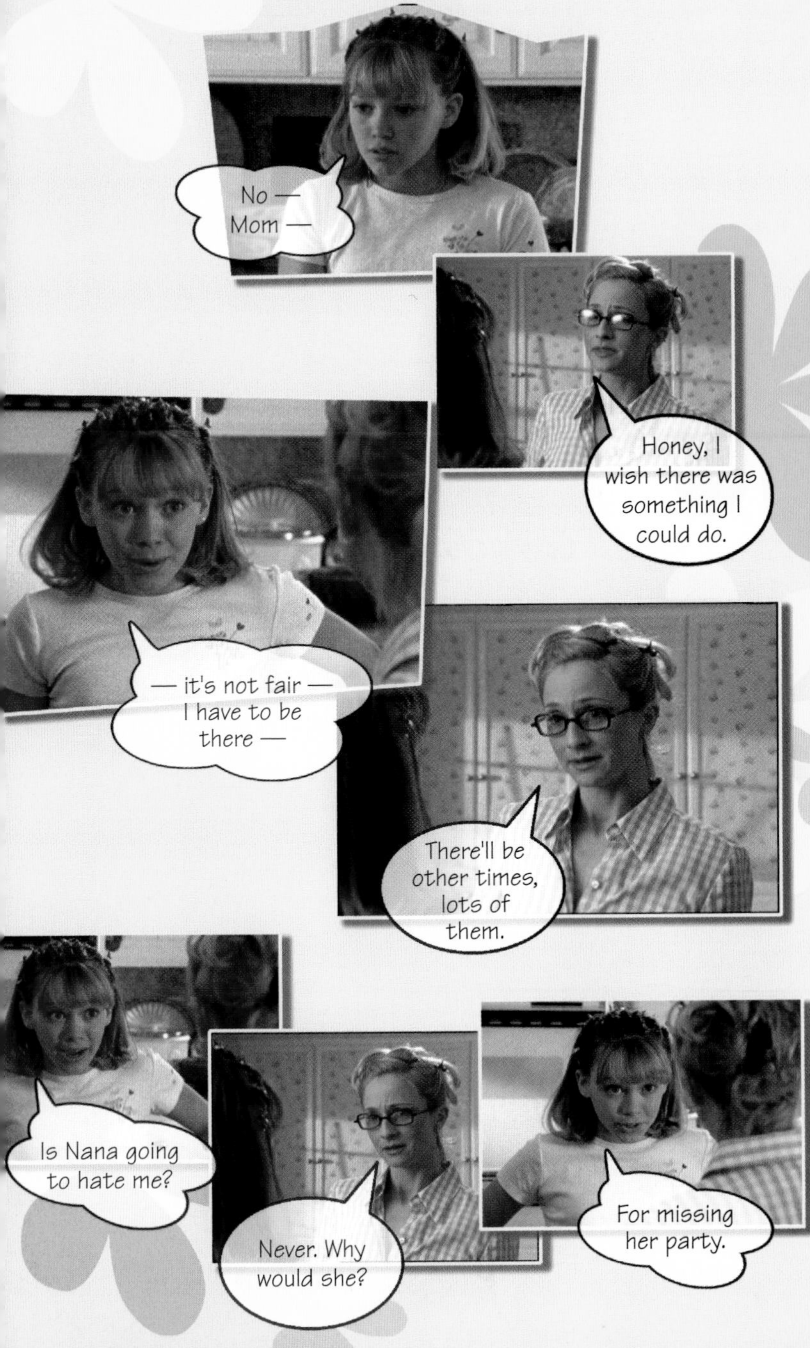
No — Mom —
Honey, I wish there was something I could do.
— it's not fair — I have to be there —
There'll be other times, lots of them.
Is Nana going to hate me?
Never. Why would she?
For missing her party.

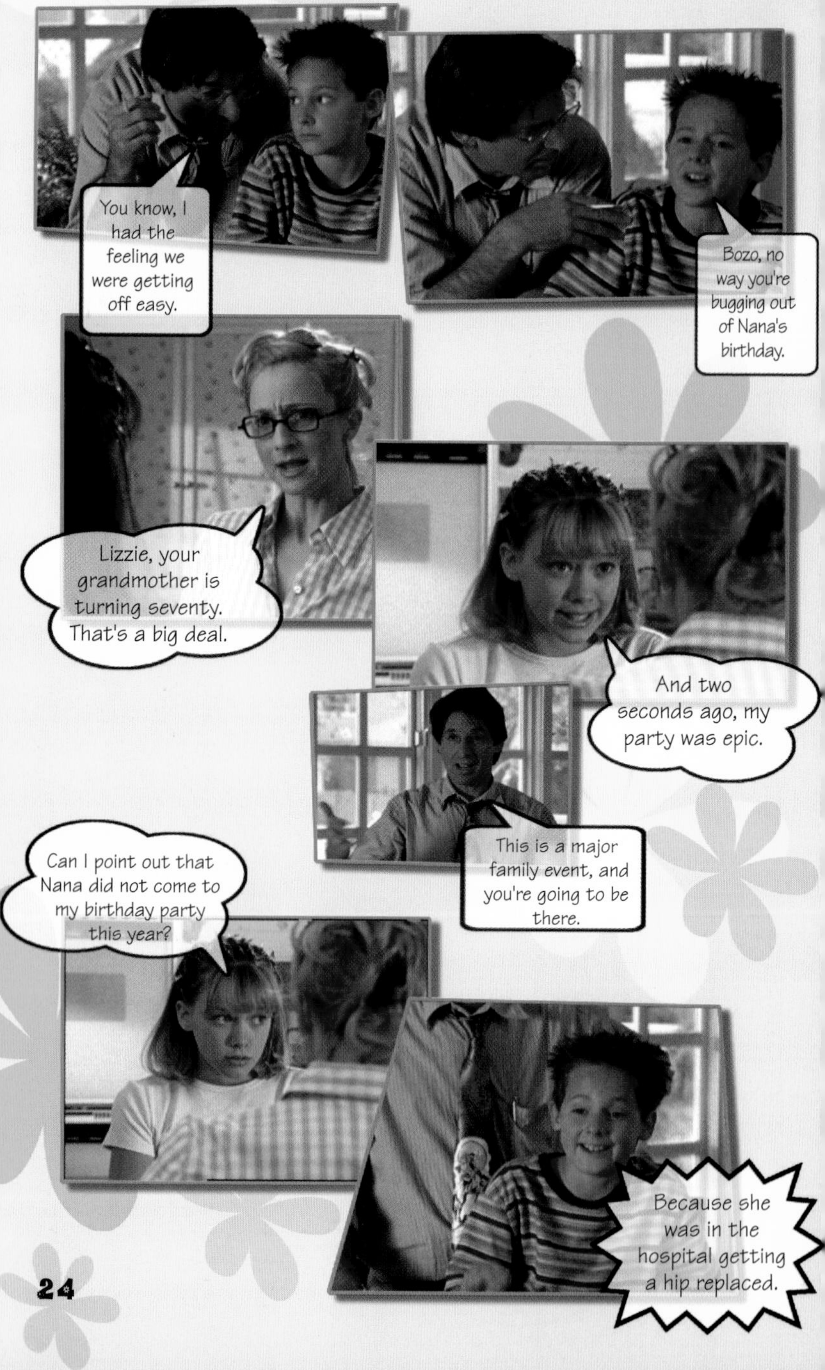
You know, I had the feeling we were getting off easy.
Bozo, no way you're bugging out of Nana's birthday.
Lizzie, your grandmother is turning seventy. That's a big deal.
And two seconds ago, my party was epic.
This is a major family event, and you're going to be there.
Can I point out that Nana did not come to my birthday party this year?
Because she was in the hospital getting a hip replaced.

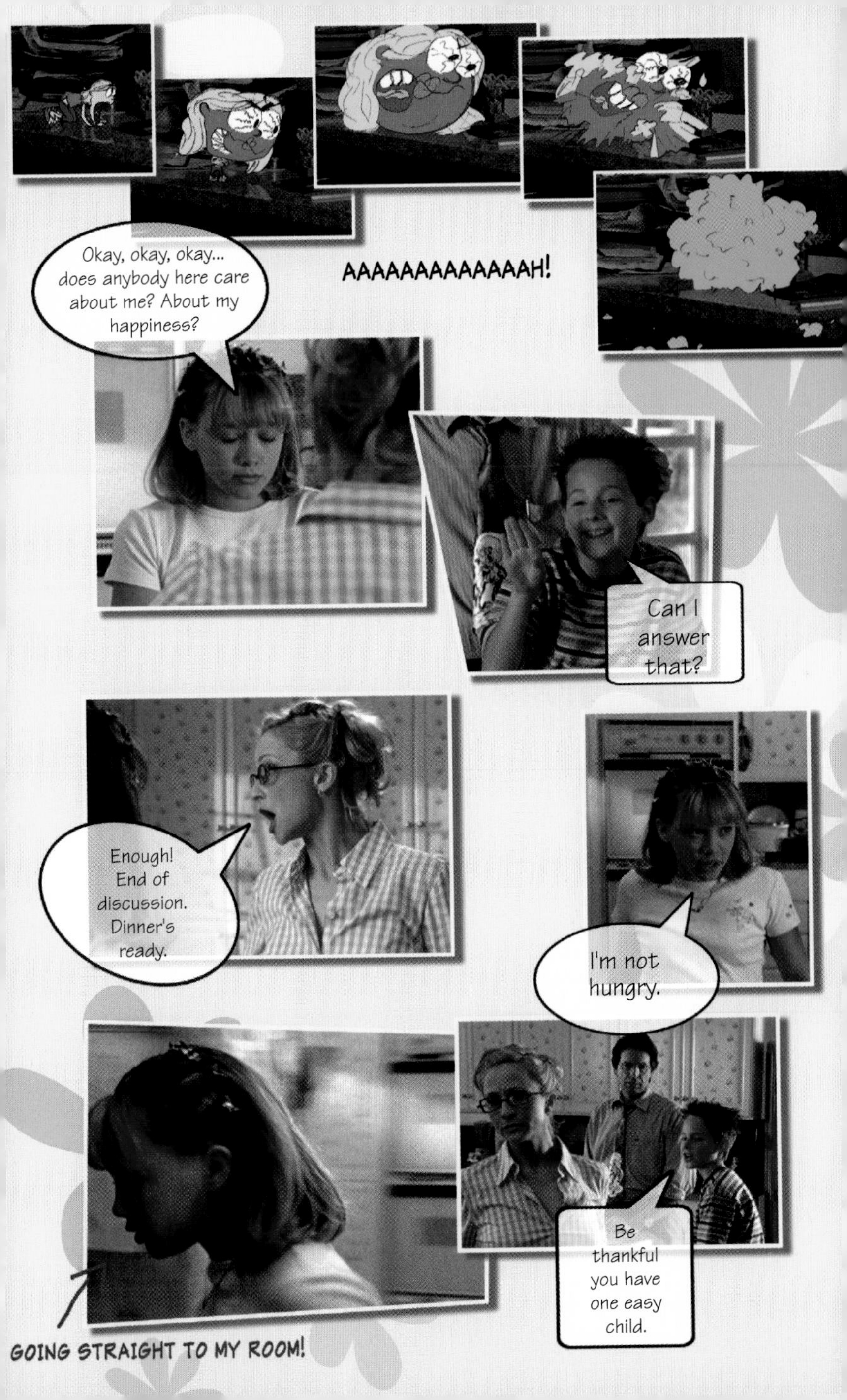
AAAAAAAAAAAAAH!
Okay, okay, okay... does anybody here care about me? About my happiness?
Can I answer that?
Enough! End of discussion. Dinner's ready.
I'm not hungry.
GOING STRAIGHT TO MY ROOM!
Be thankful you have one easy child.

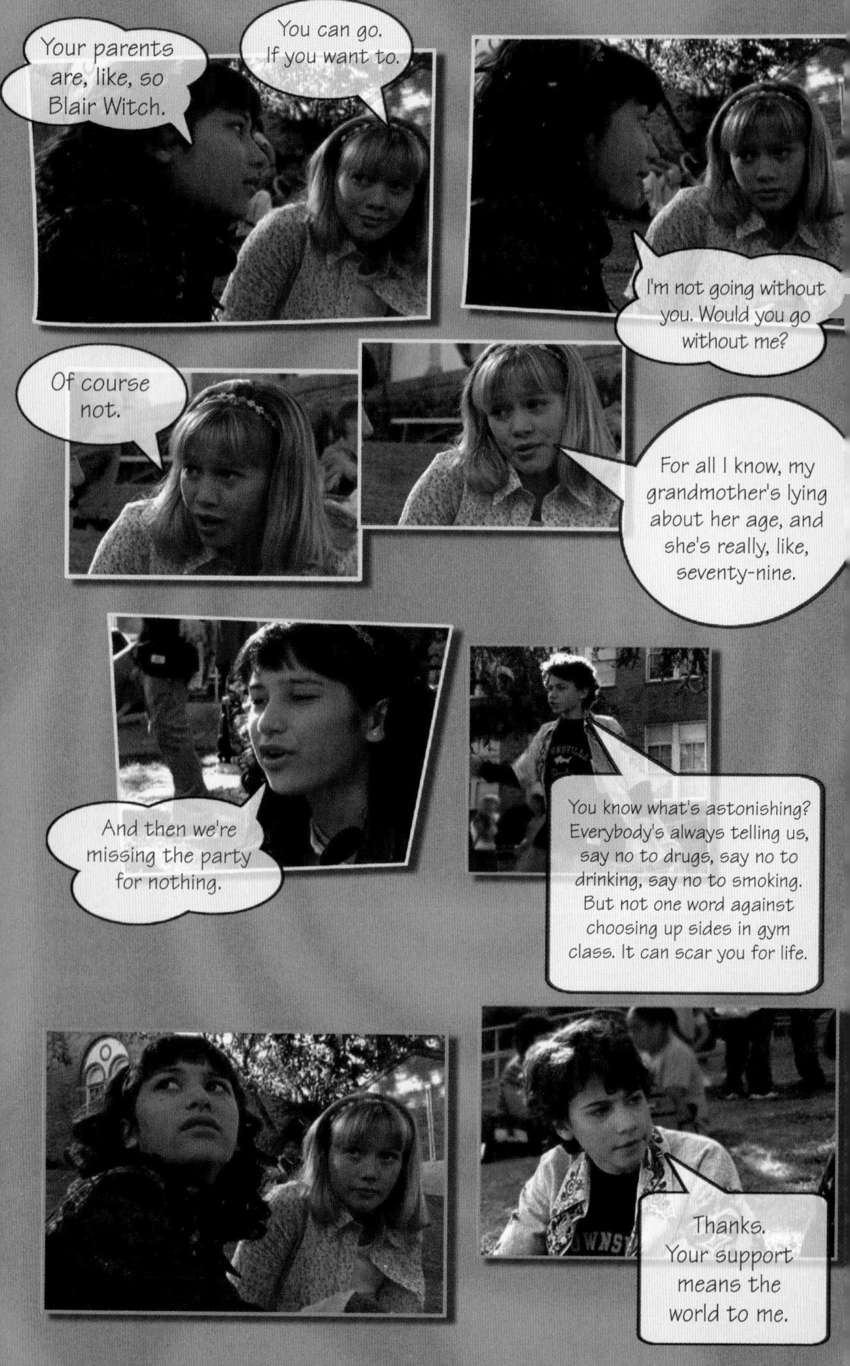
Your parents are, like, so Blair Witch.
You can go. If you want to.
I'm not going without you. Would you go without me?
Of course not.
For all I know, my grandmother's lying about her age, and she's really, like, seventy-nine.
And then we're missing the party for nothing.
You know what's astonishing? Everybody's always telling us, say no to drugs, say no to drinking, say no to smoking. But not one word against choosing up sides in gym class. It can scar you for life.
Thanks. Your support means the world to me.

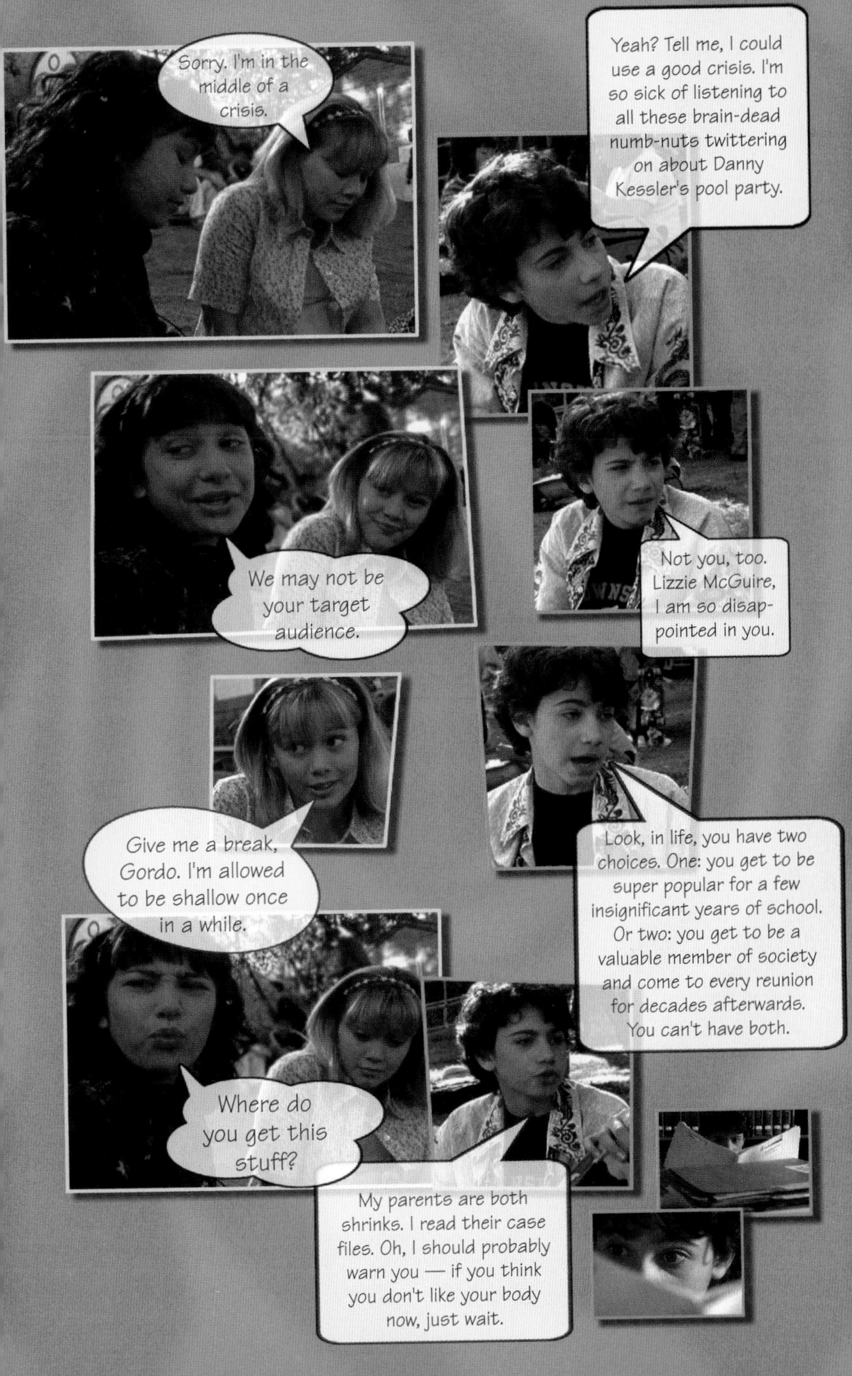
Sorry. I'm in the middle of a crisis.
Yeah? Tell me, I could use a good crisis. I'm so sick of listening to all these brain-dead numb-nuts twittering on about Danny Kessler's pool party.
We may not be your target audience.
Not you, too. Lizzie McGuire, I am so disap-pointed in you.
Give me a break, Gordo. I'm allowed to be shallow once in a while.
Look, in life, you have two choices. One: you get to be super popular for a few insignificant years of school. Or two: you get to be a valuable member of society and come to every reunion for decades afterwards. You can't have both.
Where do you get this stuff?
My parents are both shrinks. I read their case files. Oh, I should probably warn you — if you think you don't like your body now, just wait.

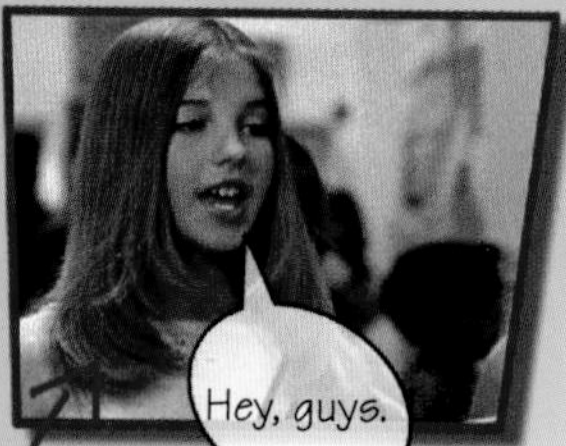
Hey, guys.

MY SCHOOL HALLWAY

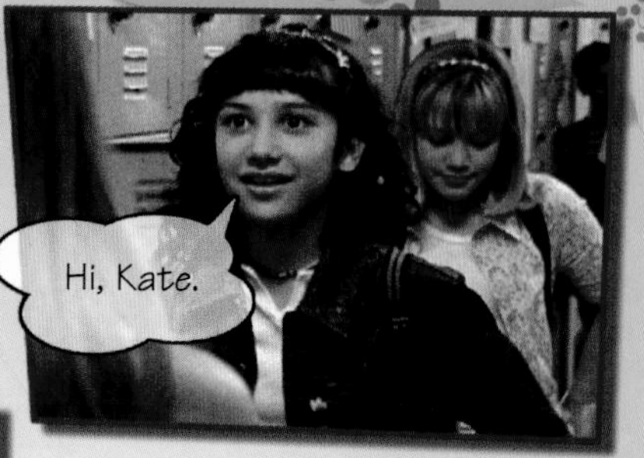
Hi, Kate.

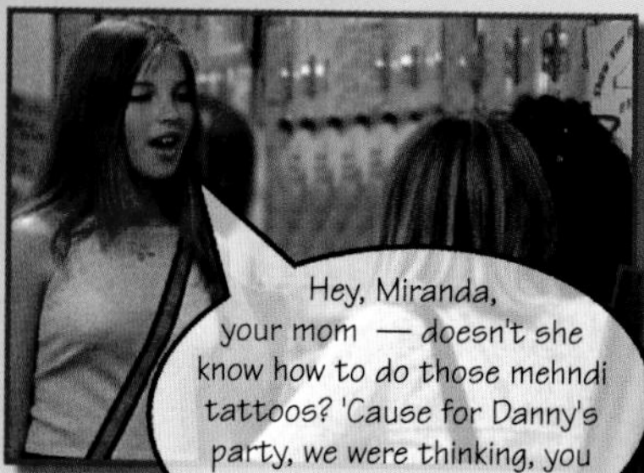
Hey, Miranda, your mom — doesn't she know how to do those mehndi tattoos? 'Cause for Danny's party, we were thinking, you know, they'd be so totally hot.

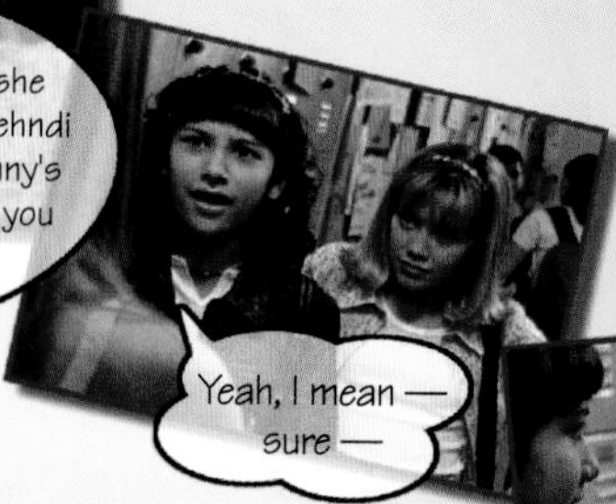
Yeah, I mean — sure —

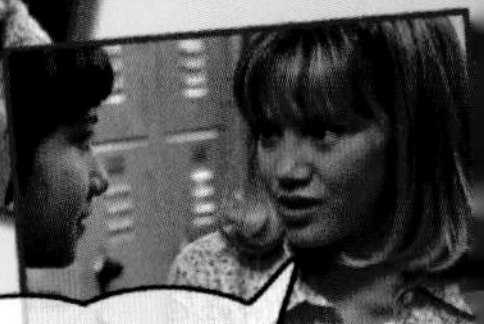
Maybe you want to ask her first.

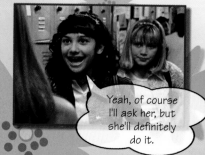

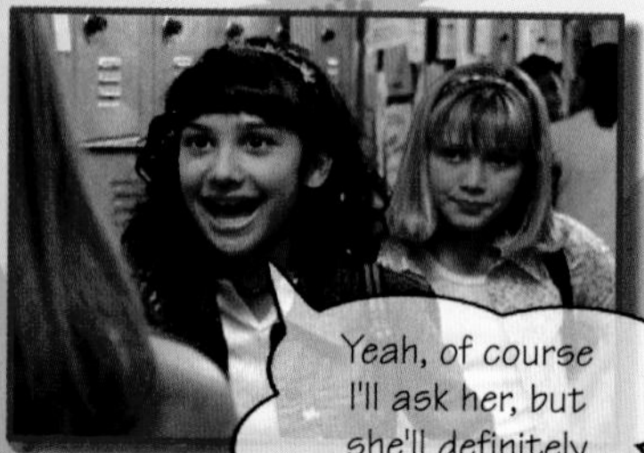
Yeah, of course I'll ask her, but she'll definitely do it.

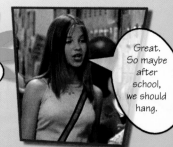

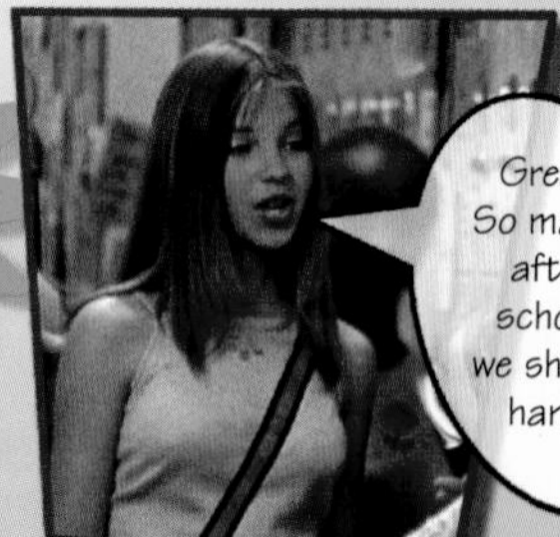
Great. So maybe after school, we should hang.

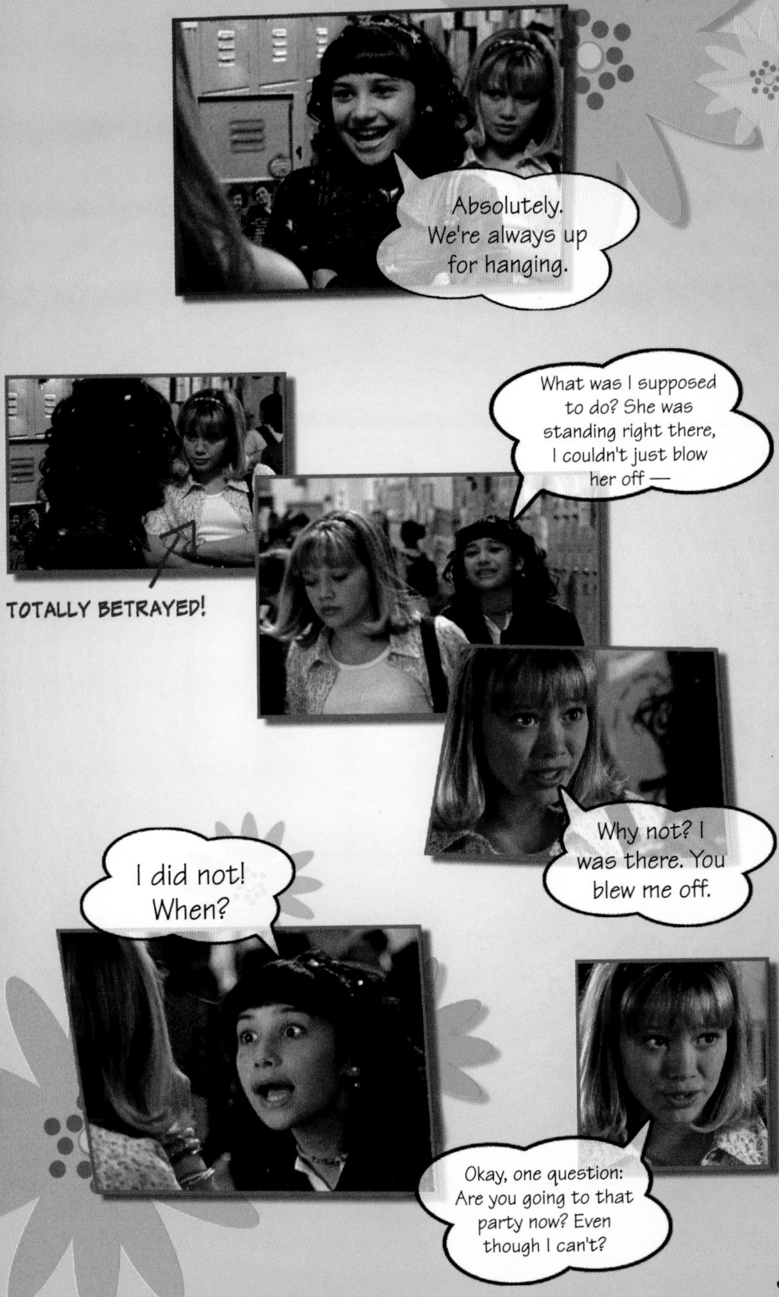
Absolutely. We're always up for hanging.
TOTALLY BETRAYED!
What was I supposed to do? She was standing right there, I couldn't just blow her off —
Why not? I was there. You blew me off.
I did not! When?
Okay, one question: Are you going to that party now? Even though I can't?

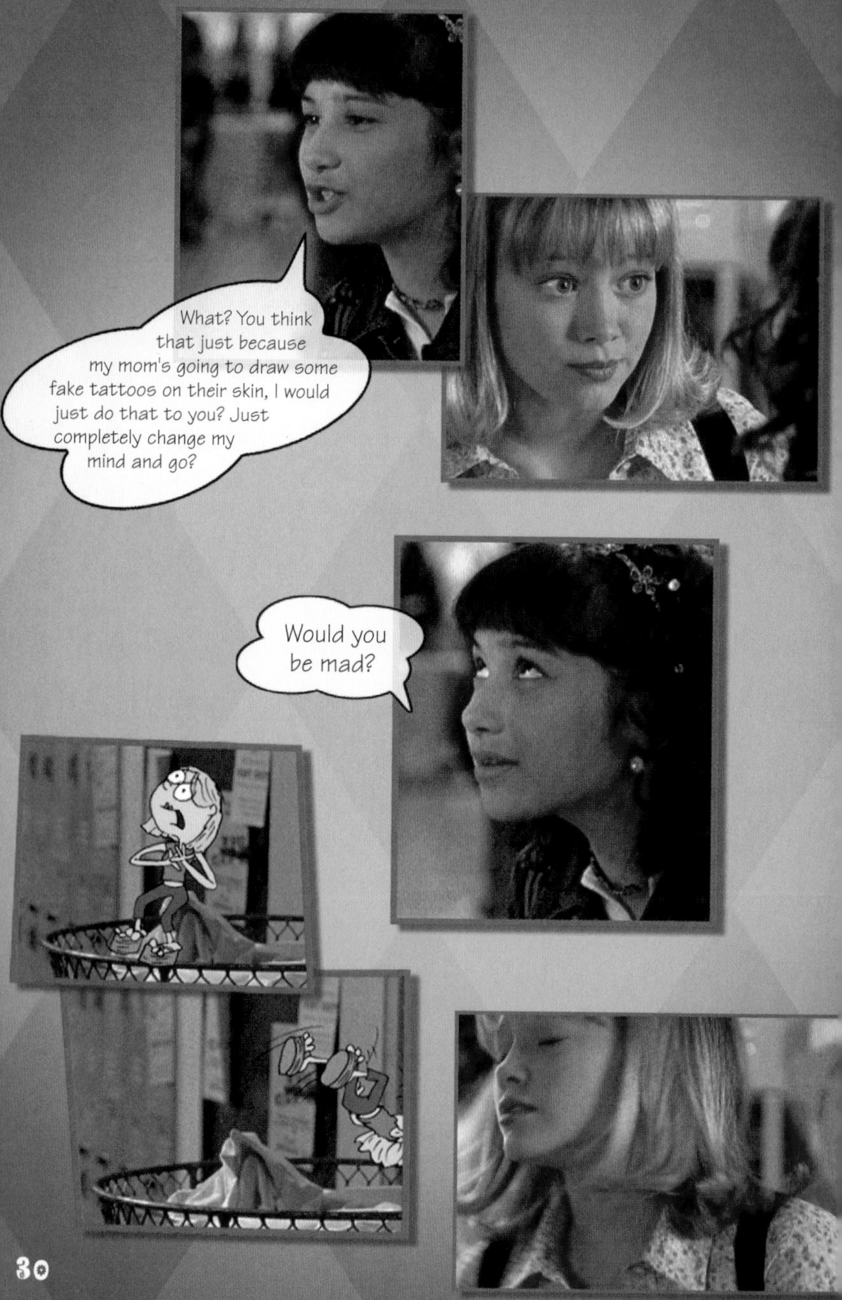
What? You think that just because my mom's going to draw some fake tattoos on their skin, I would just do that to you? Just completely change my mind and go?
Would you be mad?

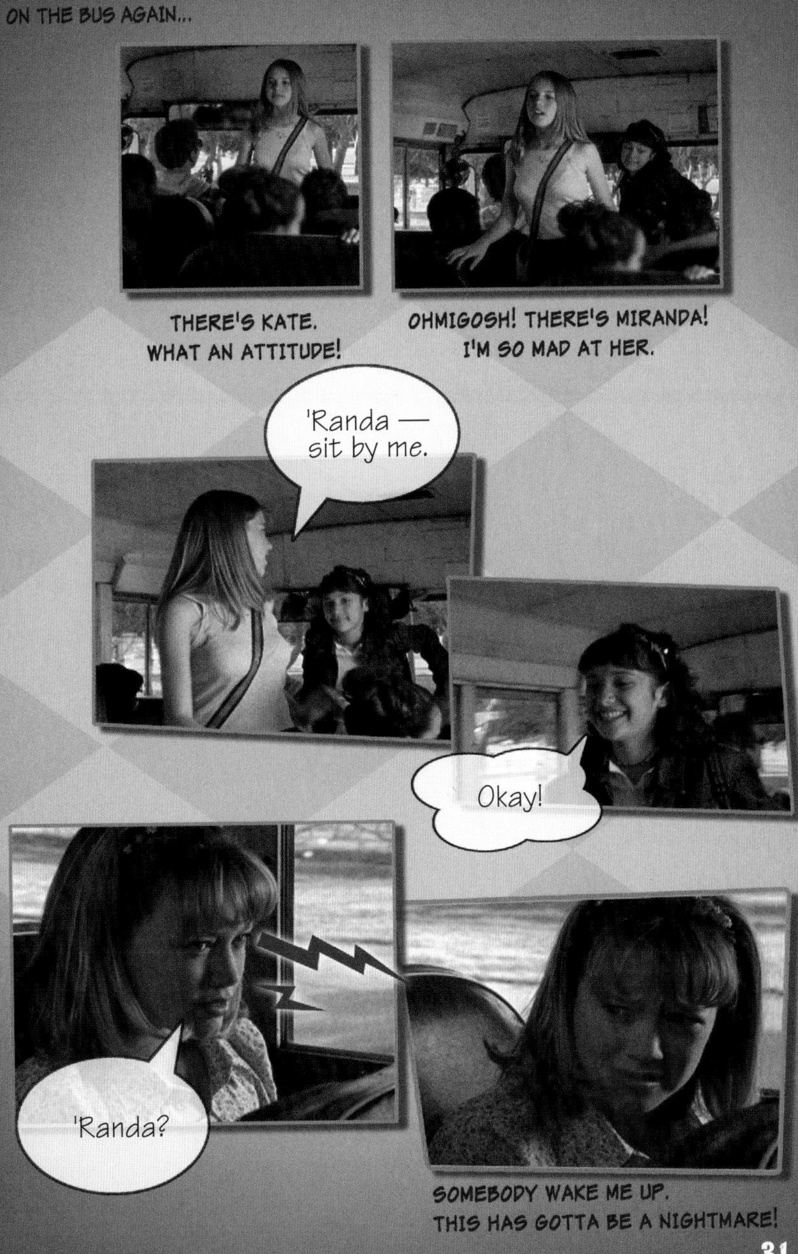
ON THE BUS AGAIN...
THERE'S KATE. WHAT AN ATTITUDE!
OHMIGOSH! THERE'S MIRANDA! I'M SO MAD AT HER.
'Randa — sit by me.
Okay!
'Randa?
SOMEBODY WAKE ME UP. THIS HAS GOTTA BE A NIGHTMARE!

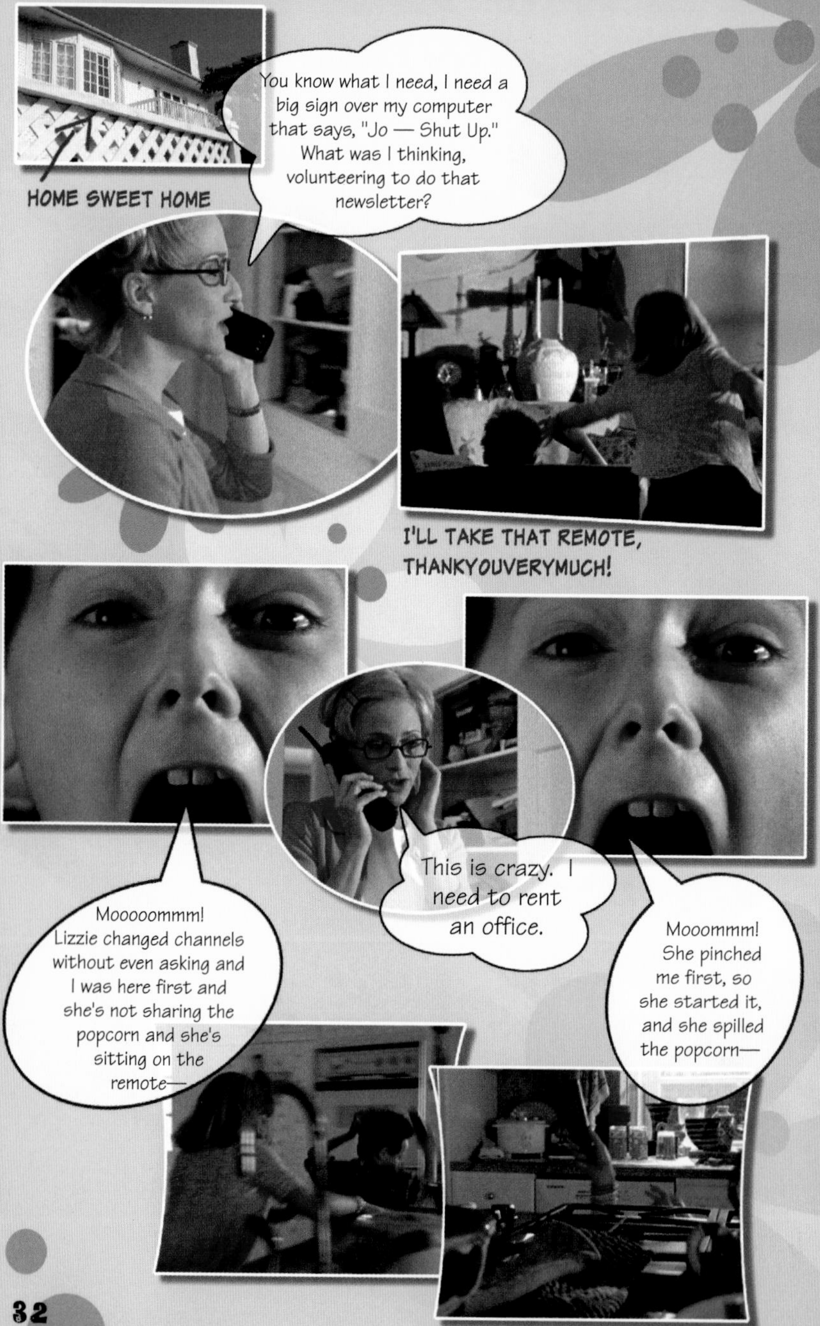
HOME SWEET HOME
You know what I need, I need a big sign over my computer that says, "Jo — Shut Up." What was I thinking, volunteering to do that newsletter?
I'LL TAKE THAT REMOTE, THANKYOUVERYMUCH!
Moooooommm! Lizzie changed channels without even asking and I was here first and she's not sharing the popcorn and she's sitting on the remote—
This is crazy. I need to rent an office.
Mooommm! She pinched me first, so she started it, and she spilled the popcorn—

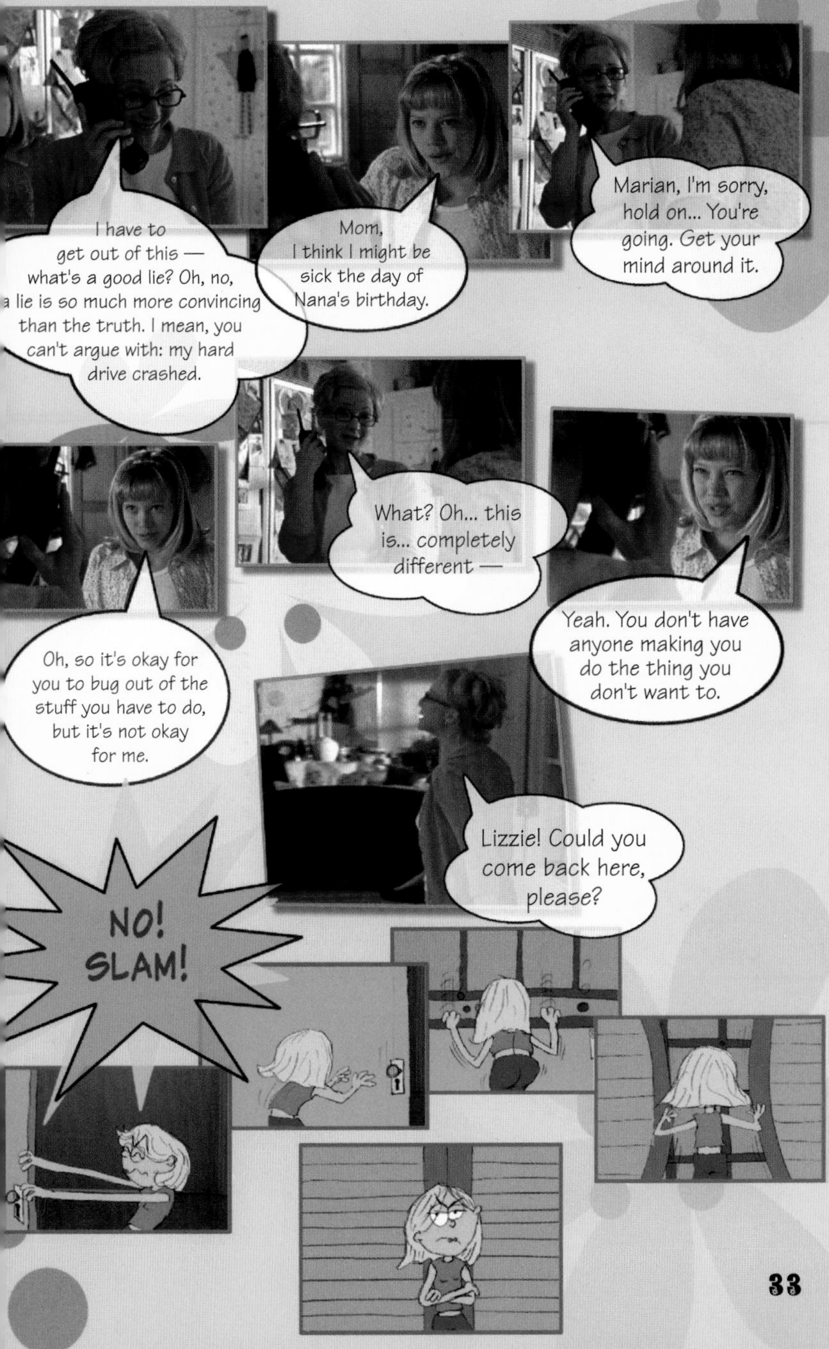

I have to get out of this — what's a good lie? Oh, no, a lie is so much more convincing than the truth. I mean, you can't argue with: my hard drive crashed.
Mom, I think I might be sick the day of Nana's birthday.
Marian, I'm sorry, hold on... You're going. Get your mind around it.
What? Oh... this is... completely different —
Oh, so it's okay for you to bug out of the stuff you have to do, but it's not okay for me.
Yeah. You don't have anyone making you do the thing you don't want to.
Lizzie! Could you come back here, please?
NO! SLAM!

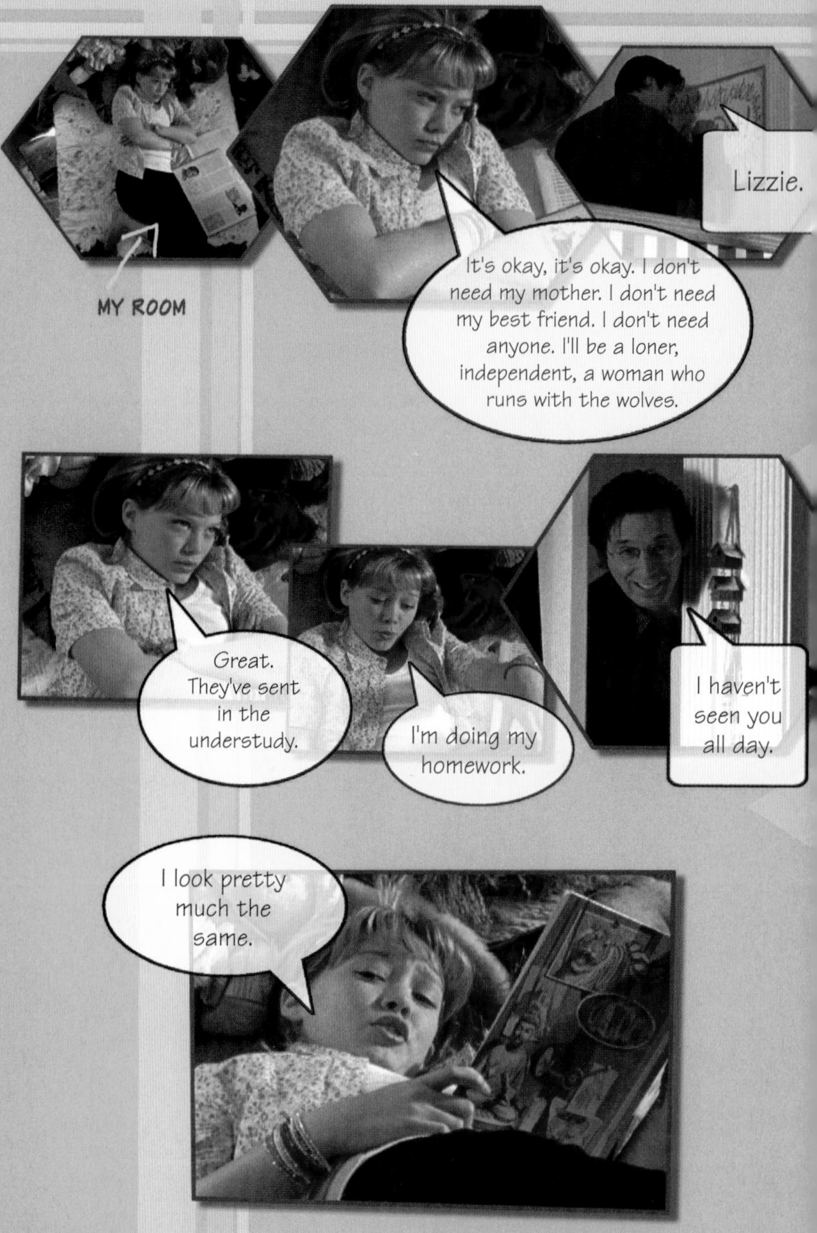
MY ROOM
It's okay, it's okay. I don't need my mother. I don't need my best friend. I don't need anyone. I'll be a loner, independent, a woman who runs with the wolves.
Lizzie.
Great. They've sent in the understudy.
I'm doing my homework.
I haven't seen you all day.
I look pretty much the same.

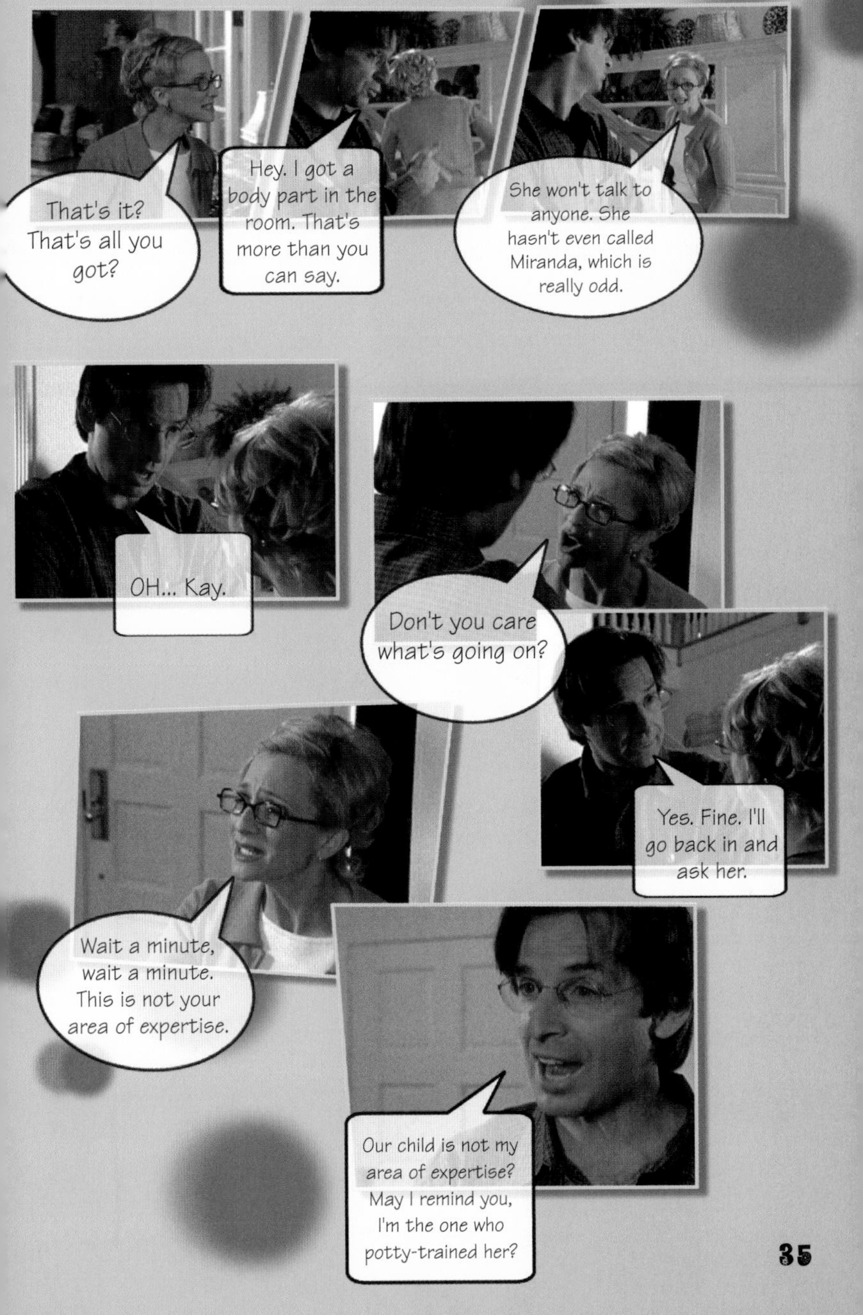
That's it? That's all you got?
Hey. I got a body part in the room. That's more than you can say.
She won't talk to anyone. She hasn't even called Miranda, which is really odd.
OH... Kay.
Don't you care what's going on?
Wait a minute, wait a minute. This is not your area of expertise.
Yes. Fine. I'll go back in and ask her.
Our child is not my area of expertise? May I remind you, I'm the one who potty-trained her?

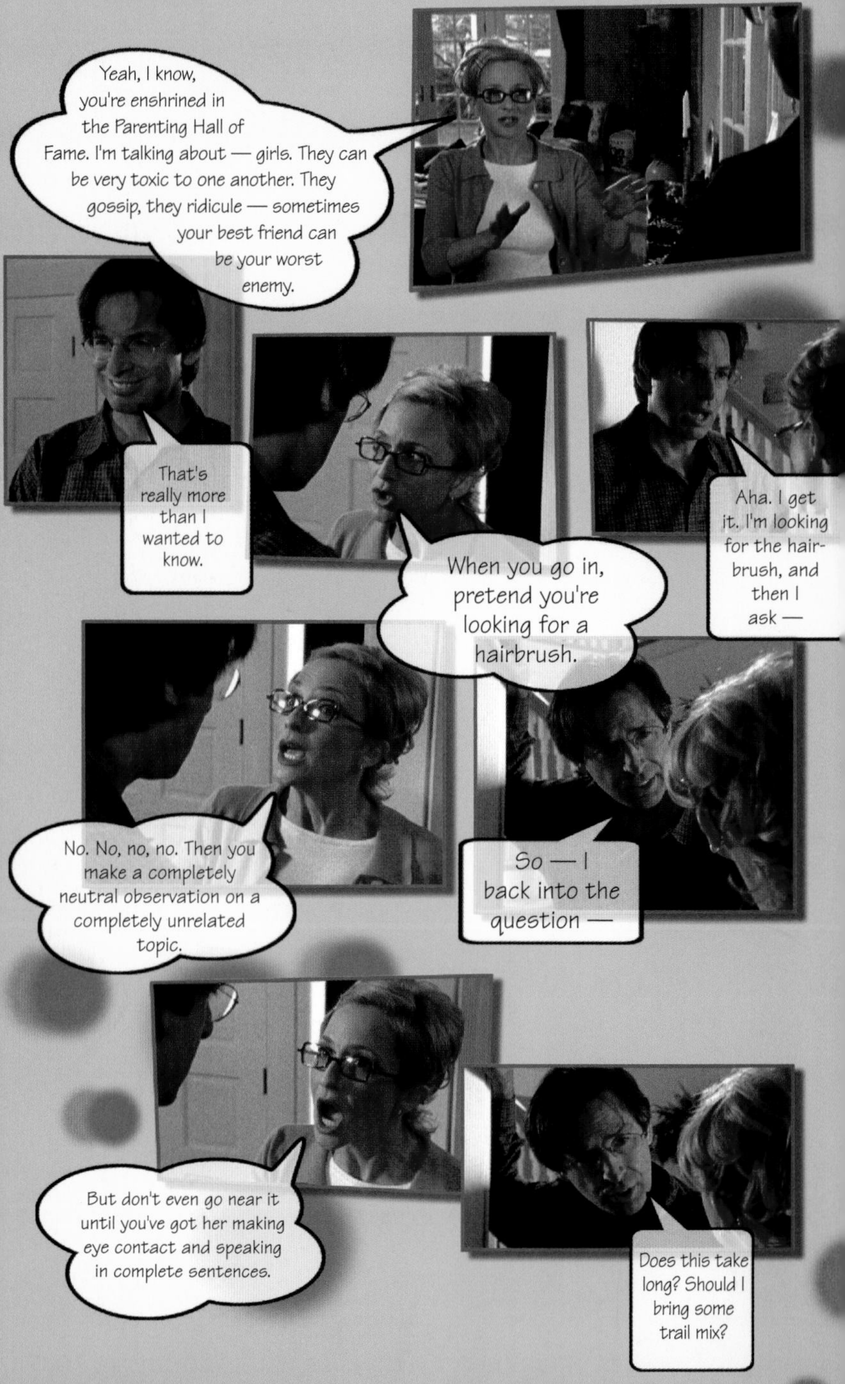
Yeah, I know, you're enshrined in the Parenting Hall of Fame. I'm talking about — girls. They can be very toxic to one another. They gossip, they ridicule — sometimes your best friend can be your worst enemy.
That's really more than I wanted to know.
When you go in, pretend you're looking for a hairbrush.
Aha. I get it. I'm looking for the hair-brush, and then I ask —
No. No, no, no. Then you make a completely neutral observation on a completely unrelated topic.
So — I back into the question —
But don't even go near it until you've got her making eye contact and speaking in complete sentences.
Does this take long? Should I bring some trail mix?

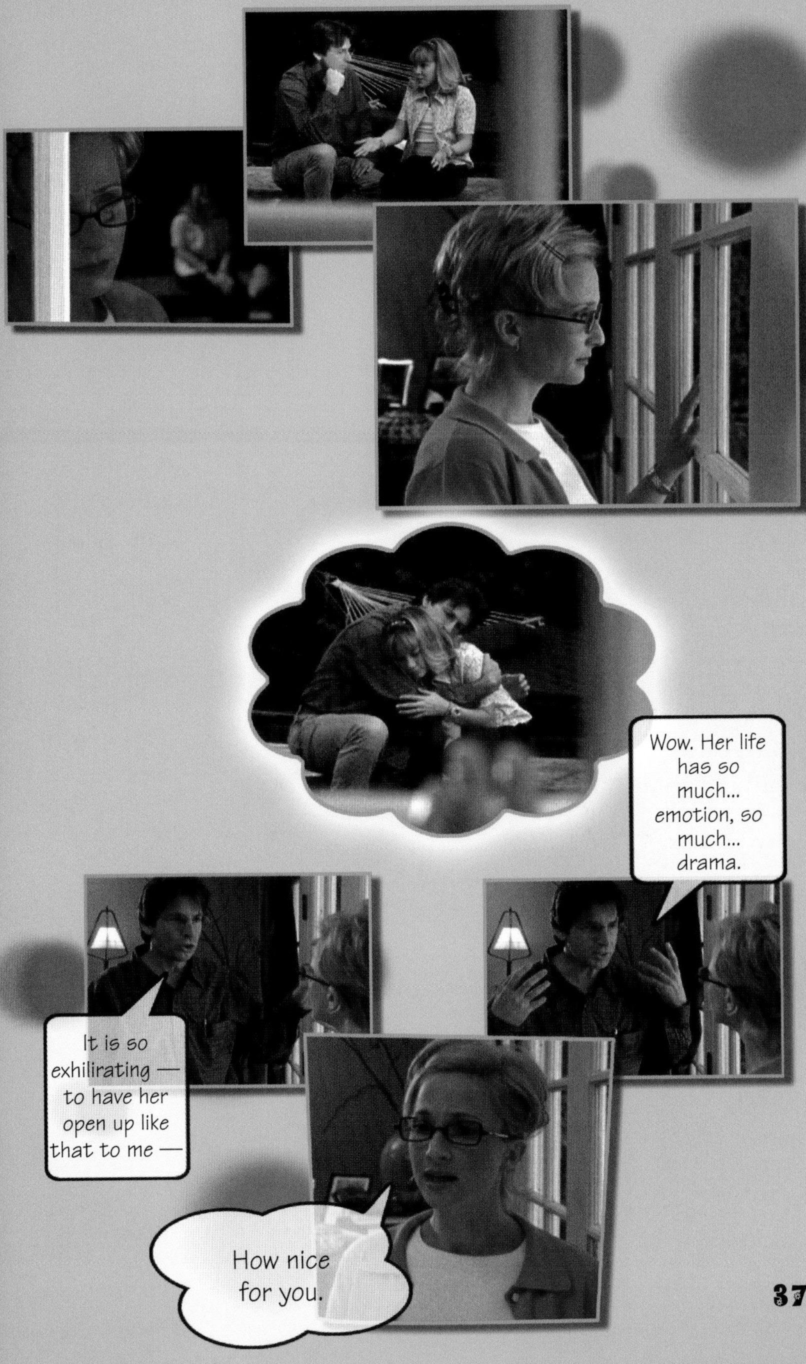
It is so exhilarating — to have her open up like that to me —
Wow. Her life has so much... emotion, so much... drama.
How nice for you.

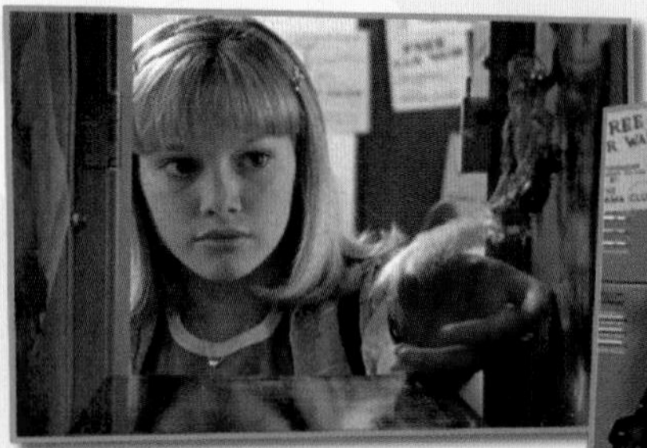

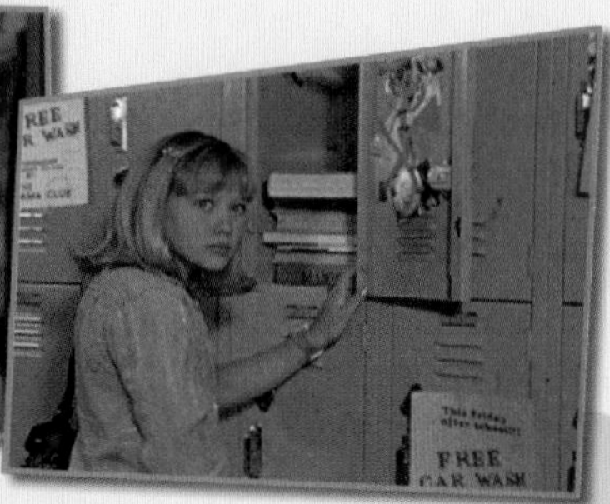
FREE
CAR WASH

BACK AT SCHOOL...

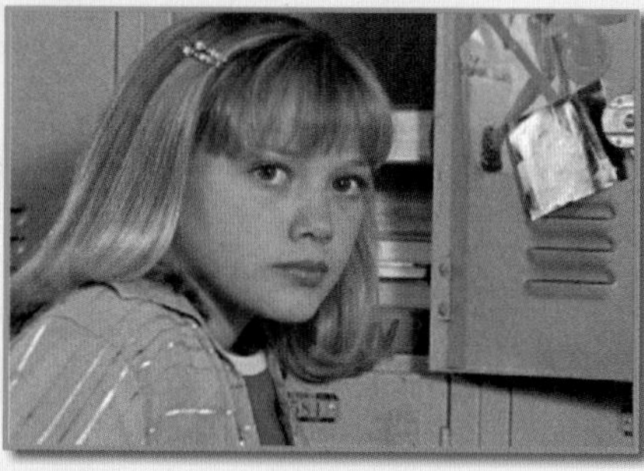

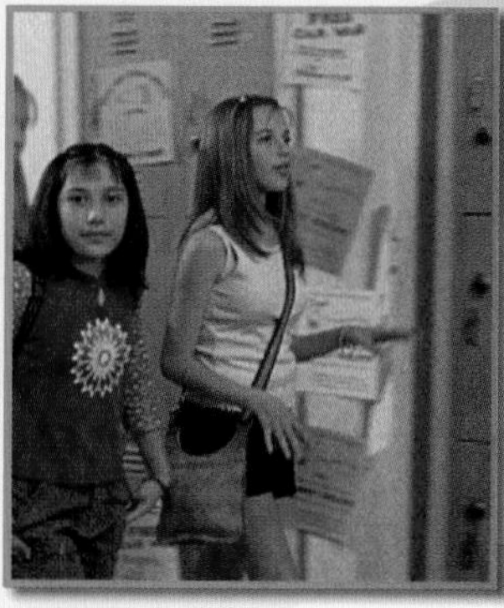

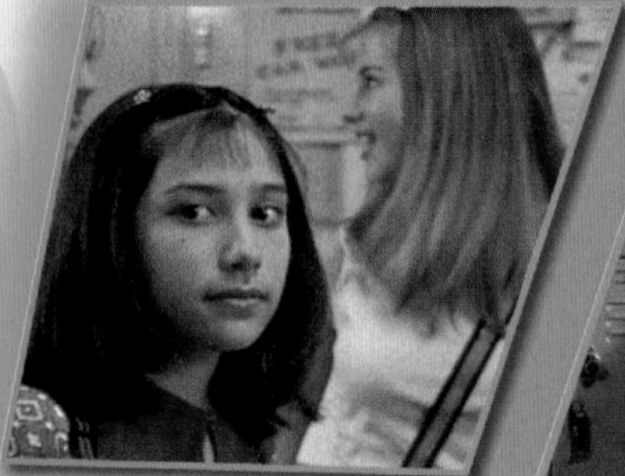

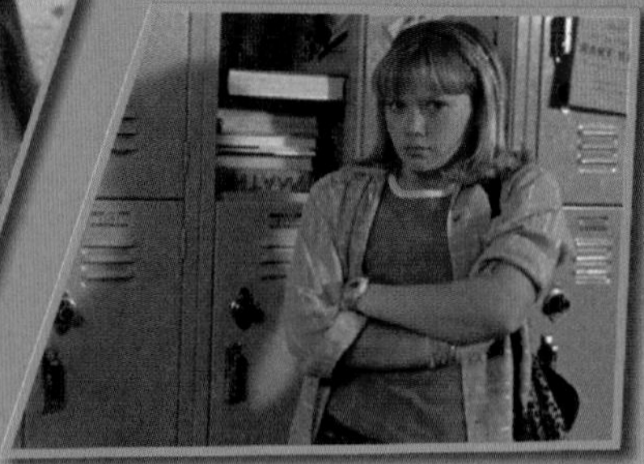

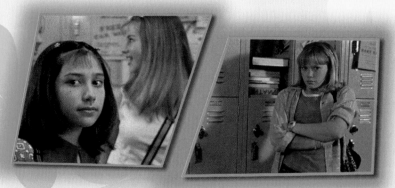

MY BEST FRIEND IS STILL BETRAYING ME...

Playing War with Gordo

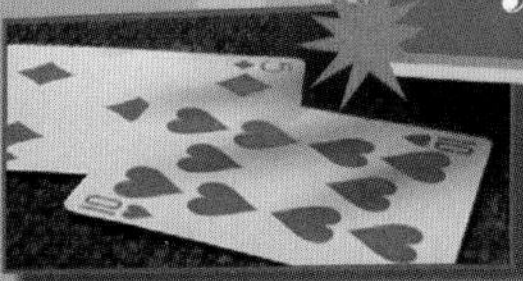

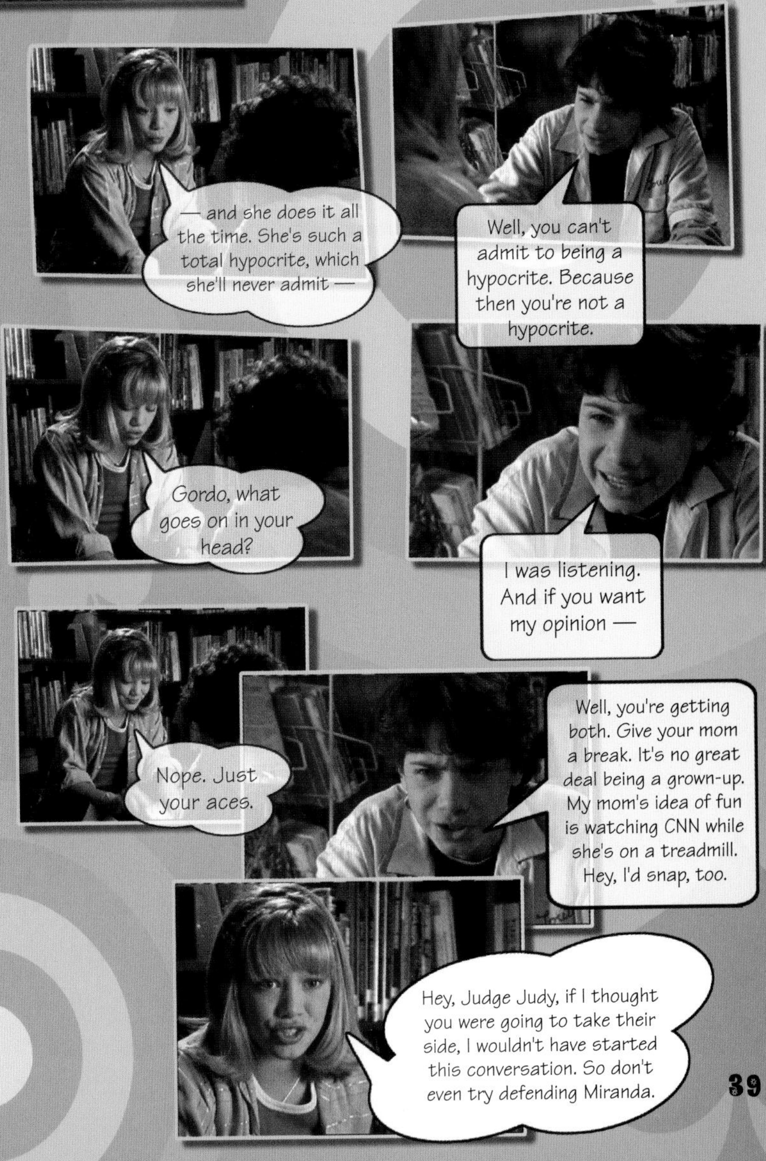
— and she does it all the time. She's such a total hypocrite, which she'll never admit —
Well, you can't admit to being a hypocrite. Because then you're not a hypocrite.
Gordo, what goes on in your head?
I was listening. And if you want my opinion —
Nope. Just your aces.
Well, you're getting both. Give your mom a break. It's no great deal being a grown-up. My mom's idea of fun is watching CNN while she's on a treadmill. Hey, I'd snap, too.
Hey, Judge Judy, if I thought you were going to take their side, I wouldn't have started this conversation. So don't even try defending Miranda.

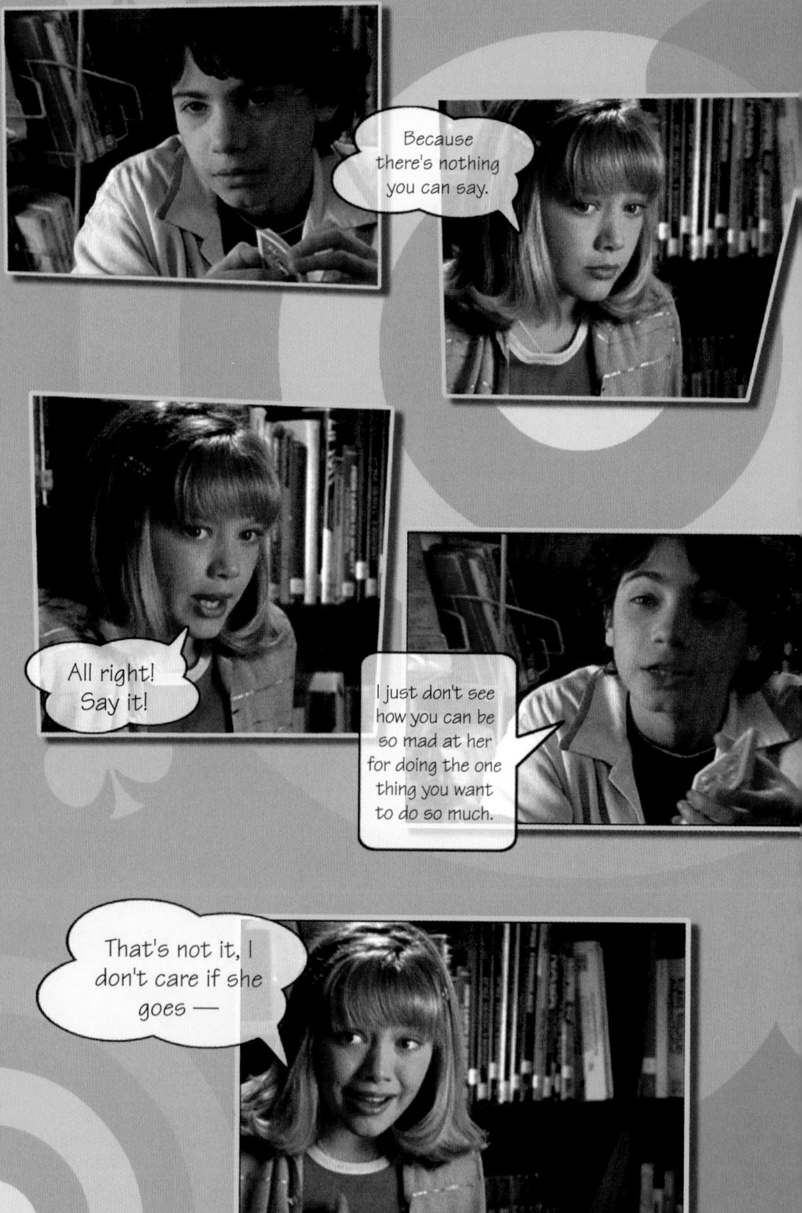
Because there's nothing you can say.
All right! Say it!
I just don't see how you can be so mad at her for doing the one thing you want to do so much.
That's not it, I don't care if she goes —

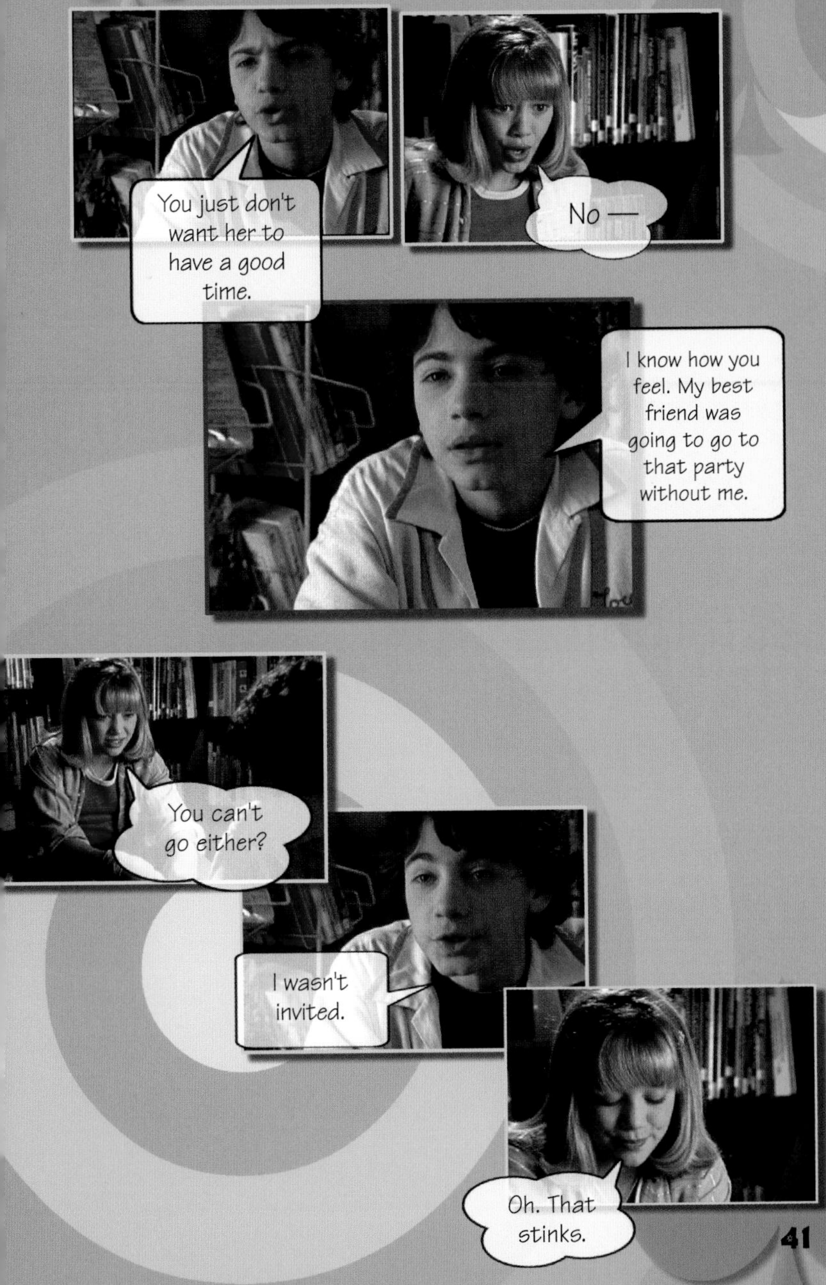
You just don't want her to have a good time.
No —
I know how you feel. My best friend was going to go to that party without me.
You can't go either?
I wasn't invited.
Oh. That stinks.

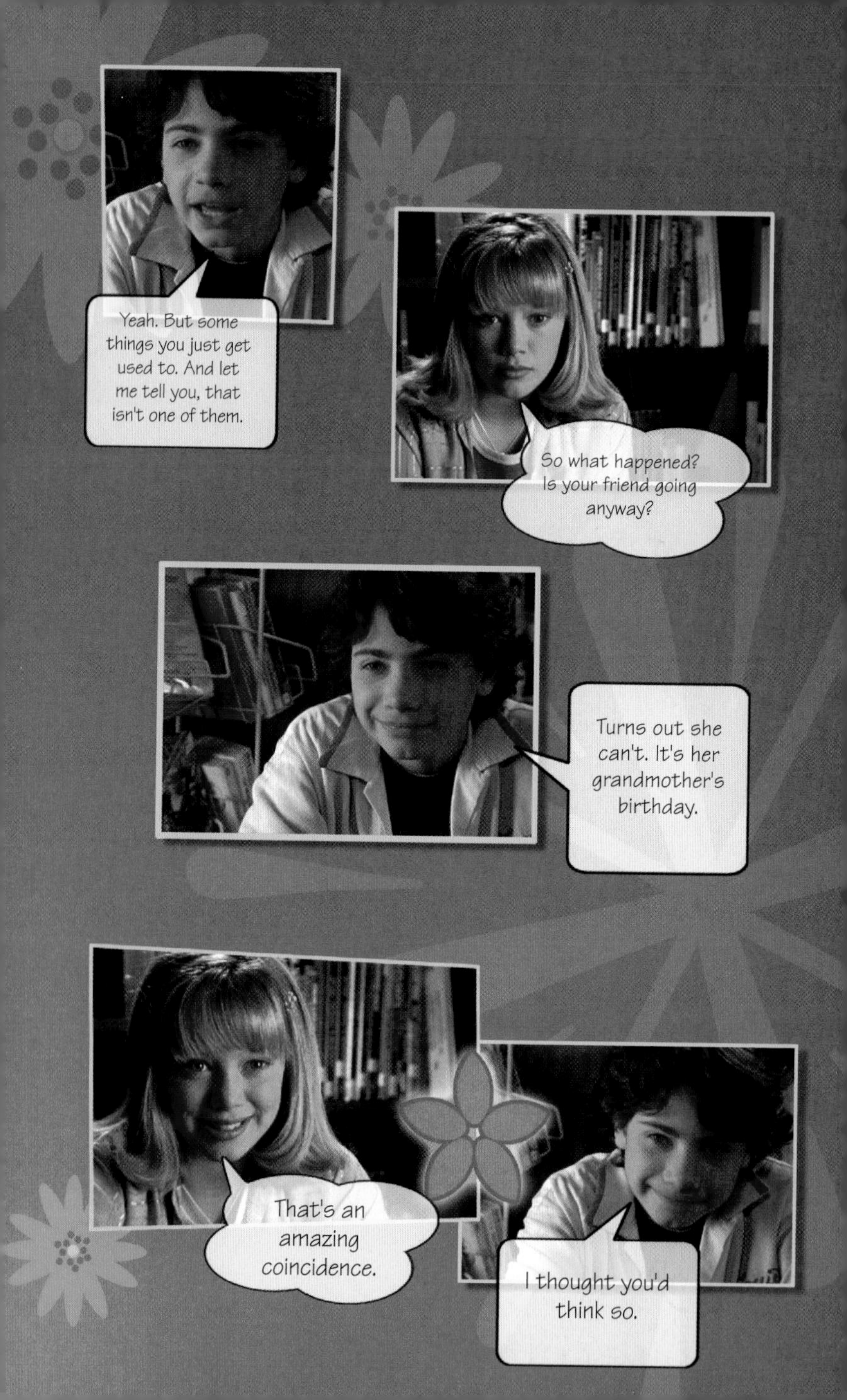
Yeah. But some things you just get used to. And let me tell you, that isn't one of them.
So what happened? Is your friend going anyway?
Turns out she can't. It's her grandmother's birthday.
That's an amazing coincidence.
I thought you'd think so.

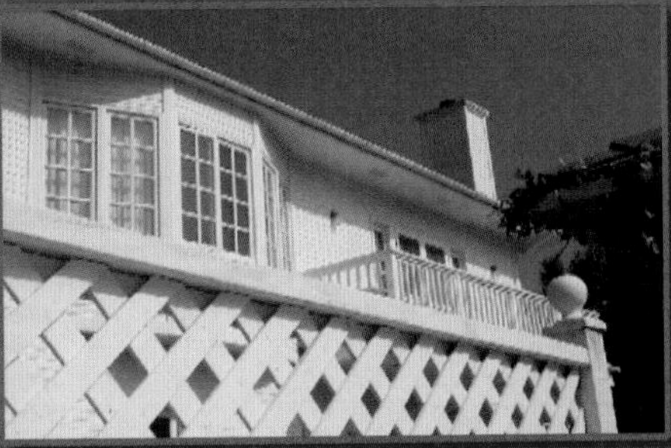

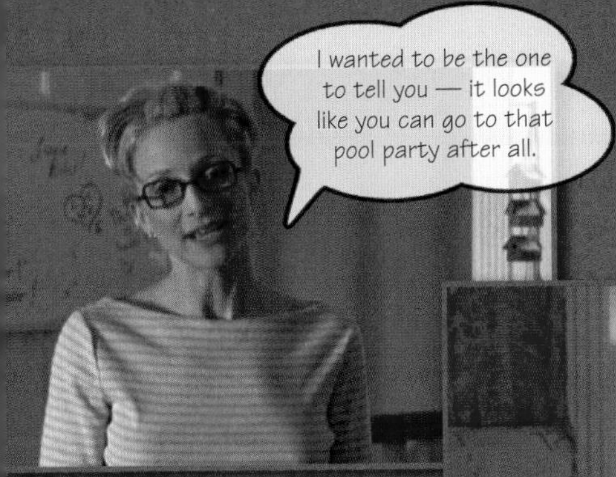
I wanted to be the one to tell you — it looks like you can go to that pool party after all.

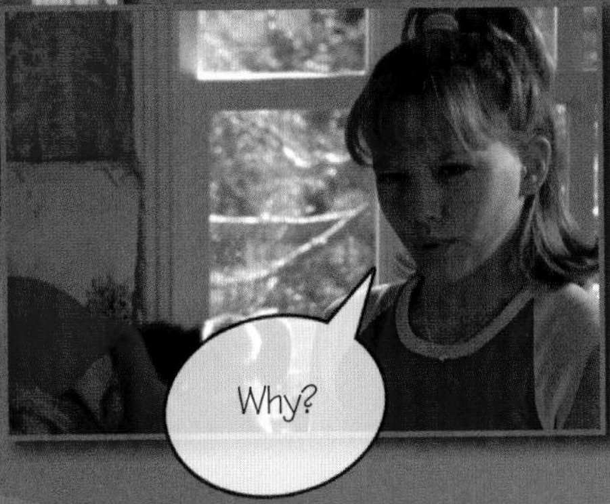
Why?

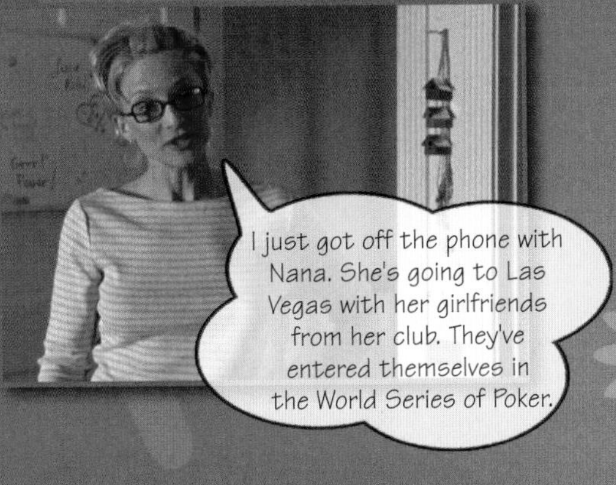
I just got off the phone with Nana. She's going to Las Vegas with her girlfriends from her club. They've entered themselves in the World Series of Poker.

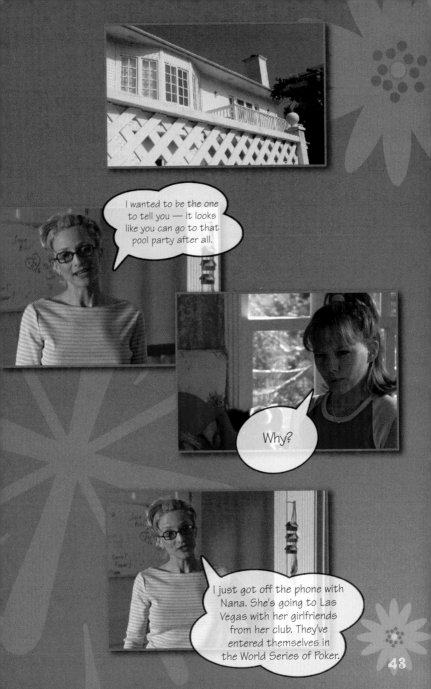

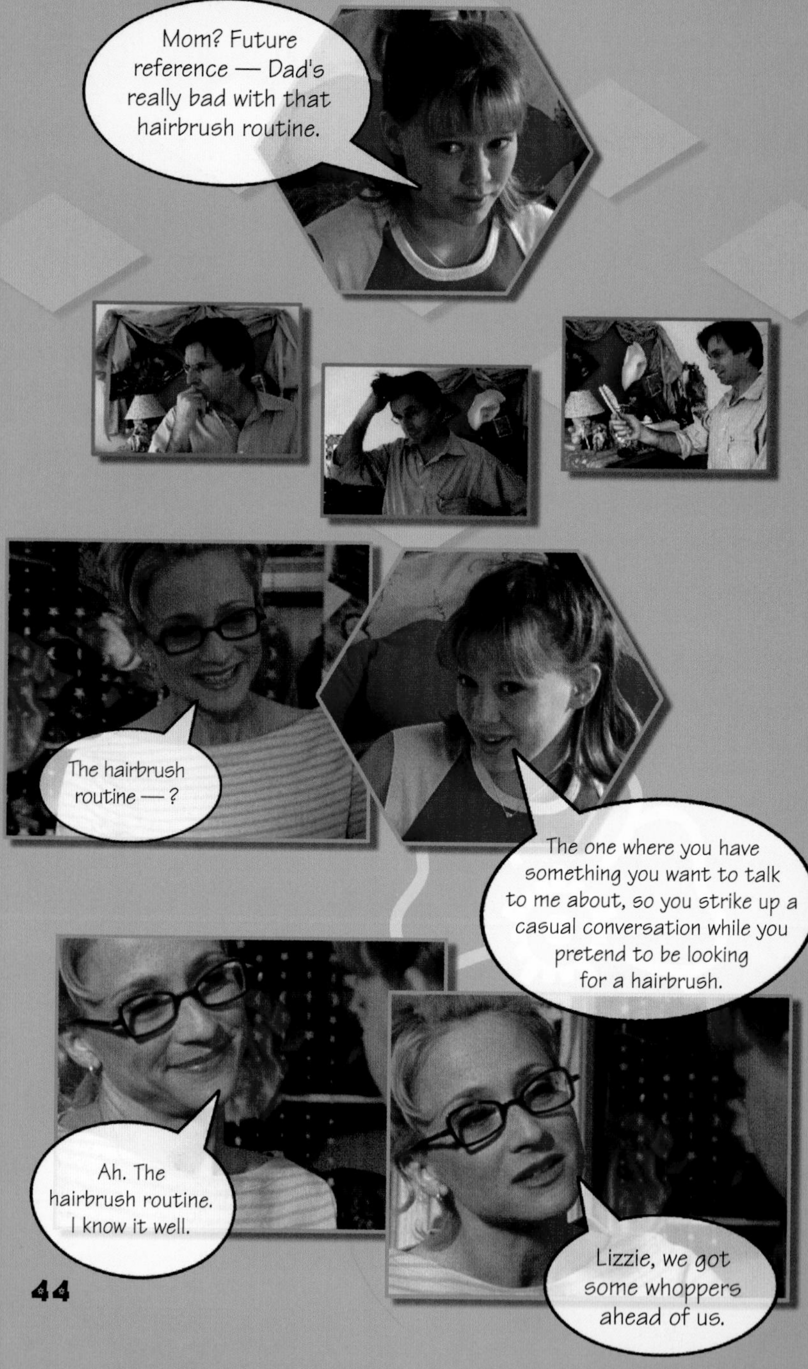
Mom? Future reference — Dad's really bad with that hairbrush routine.
The hairbrush routine — ?
The one where you have something you want to talk to me about, so you strike up a casual conversation while you pretend to be looking for a hairbrush.
Ah. The hairbrush routine. I know it well.
Lizzie, we got some whoppers ahead of us.

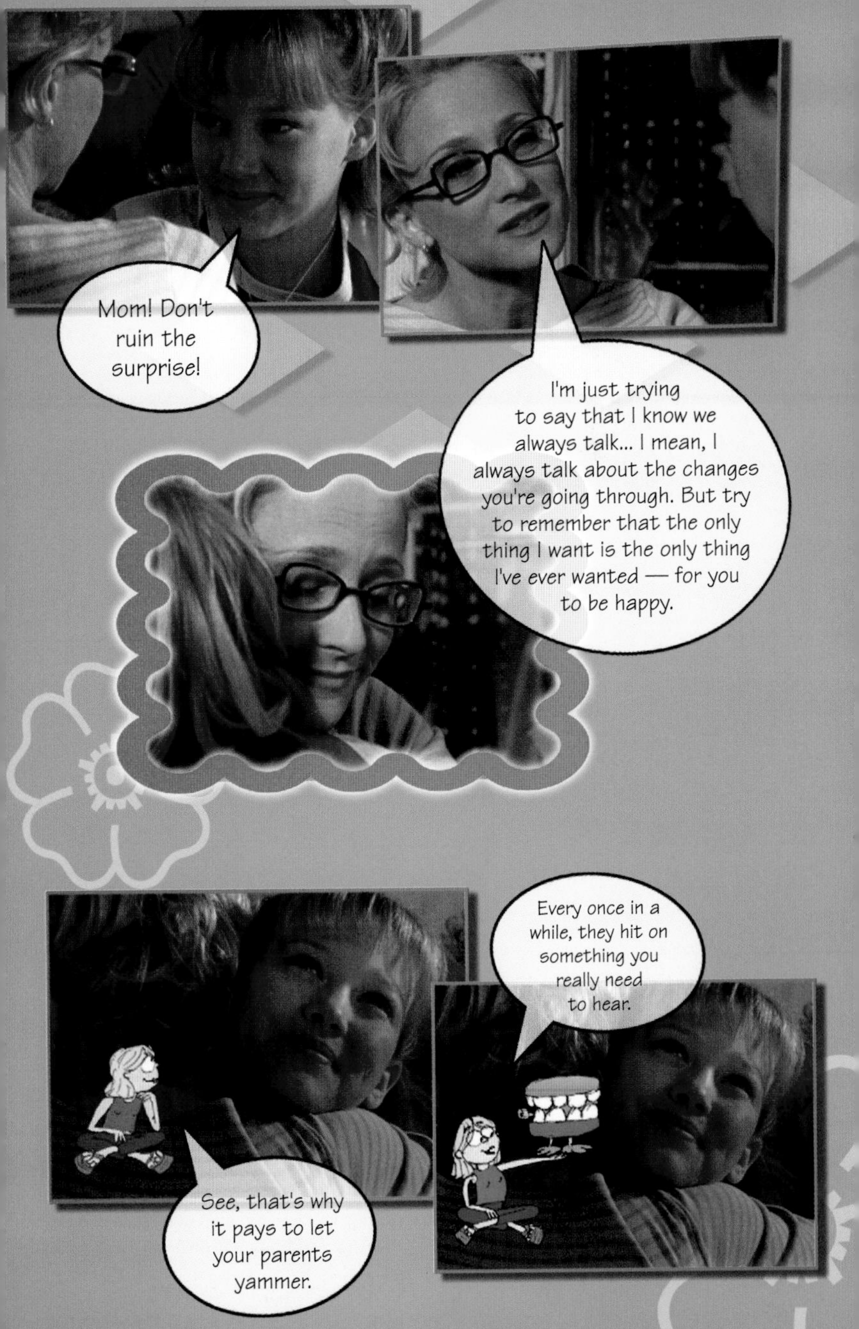
Mom! Don't ruin the surprise!
I'm just trying to say that I know we always talk... I mean, I always talk about the changes you're going through. But try to remember that the only thing I want is the only thing I've ever wanted — for you to be happy.
See, that's why it pays to let your parents yammer.
Every once in a while, they hit on something you really need to hear.

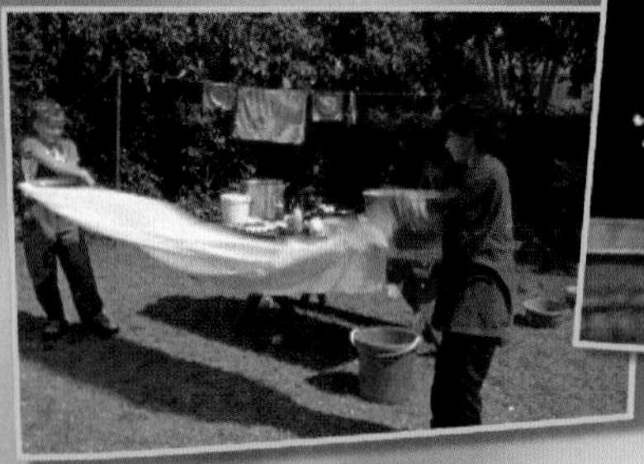
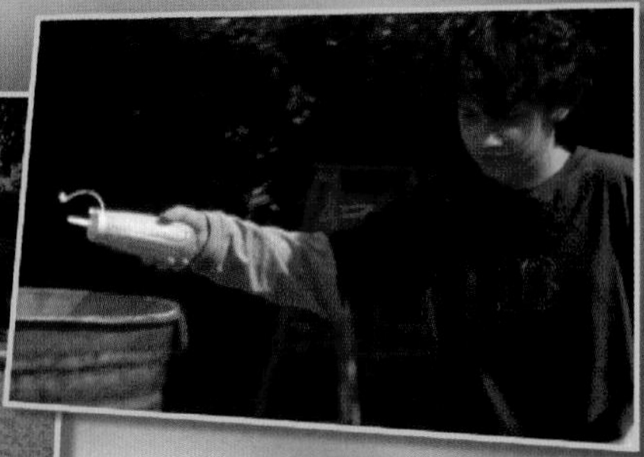
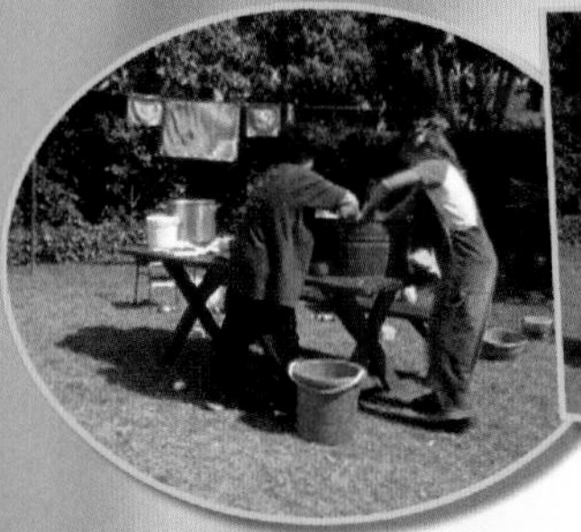
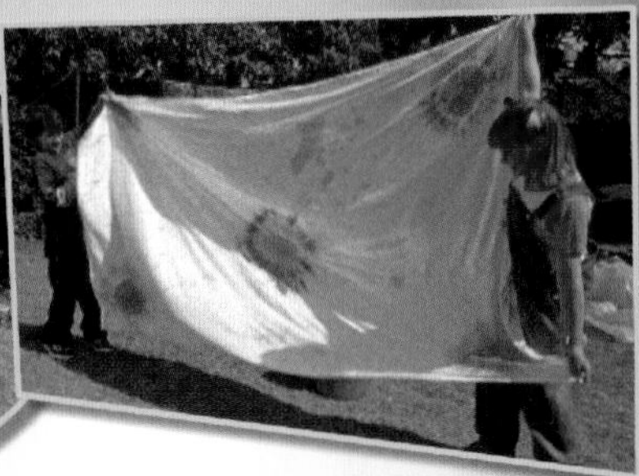
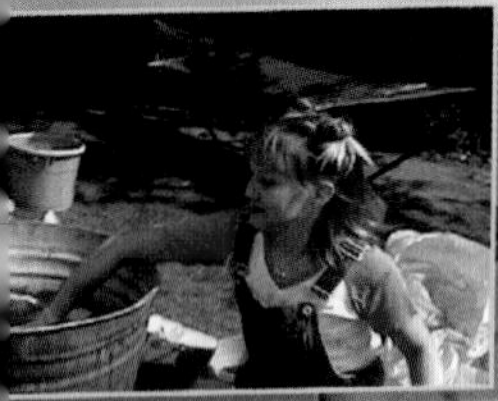
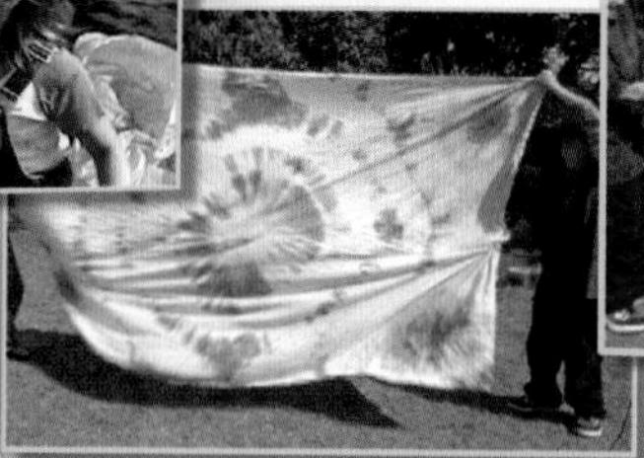
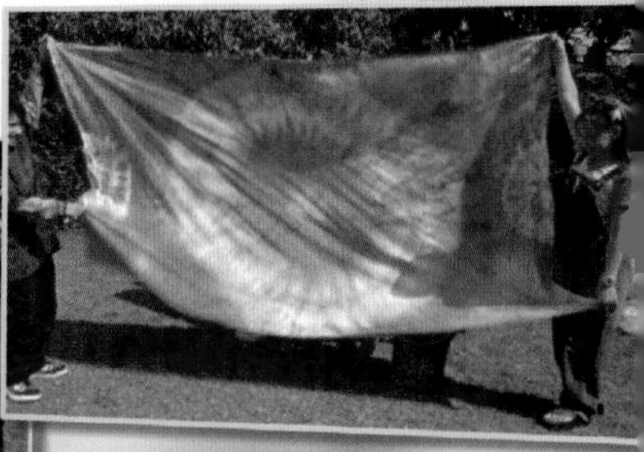

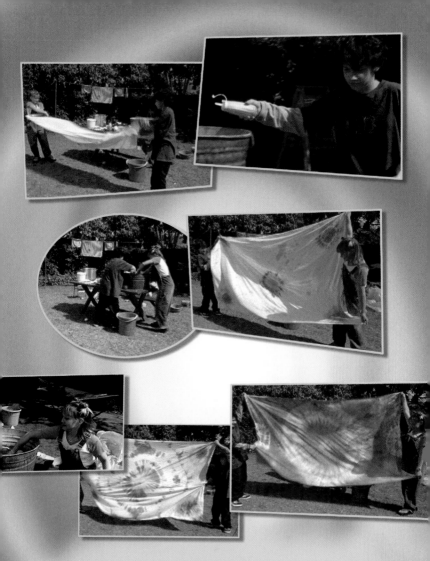

AS IT TURNS OUT, I DECIDED NOT TO GO TO DANNY KESSLER'S PARTY. GORDO SAYS IT'S ALWAYS USEFUL TO CONFOUND YOUR PEERS BY NOT DOING THE THING THAT'S EXPECTED OF YOU. I HAVE NO IDEA IF HE'S RIGHT, BUT I FIGURE, IF YOU'RE GOING TO LISTEN TO ANYBODY, MIGHT AS WELL BE A GUY WHO SPENDS THE WHOLE DAY HELPING YOU TIE-DYE YOUR SHEETS.

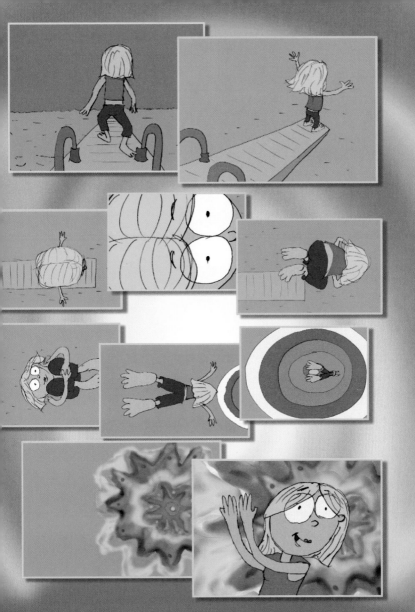

SO — MAYBE I MISSED THE DEFINING EVENT OF MY ADOLESCENCE. BUT, THEN AGAIN, MAYBE THE DEFINING MOMENT IS REALIZING THAT THERE IS NO SUCH THING. YEAH, THAT'S IT.

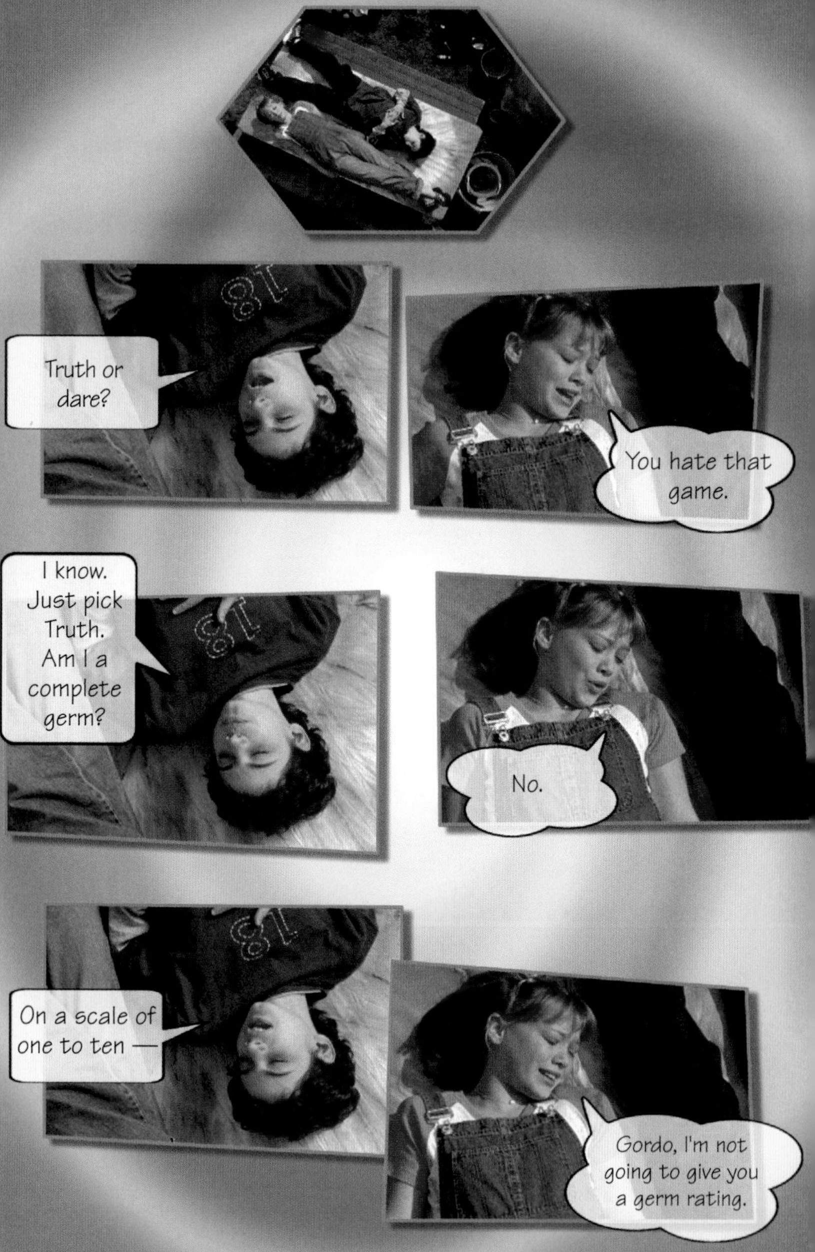
Truth or dare?
You hate that game.
I know. Just pick Truth. Am I a complete germ?
No.
On a scale of one to ten —
Gordo, I'm not going to give you a germ rating.

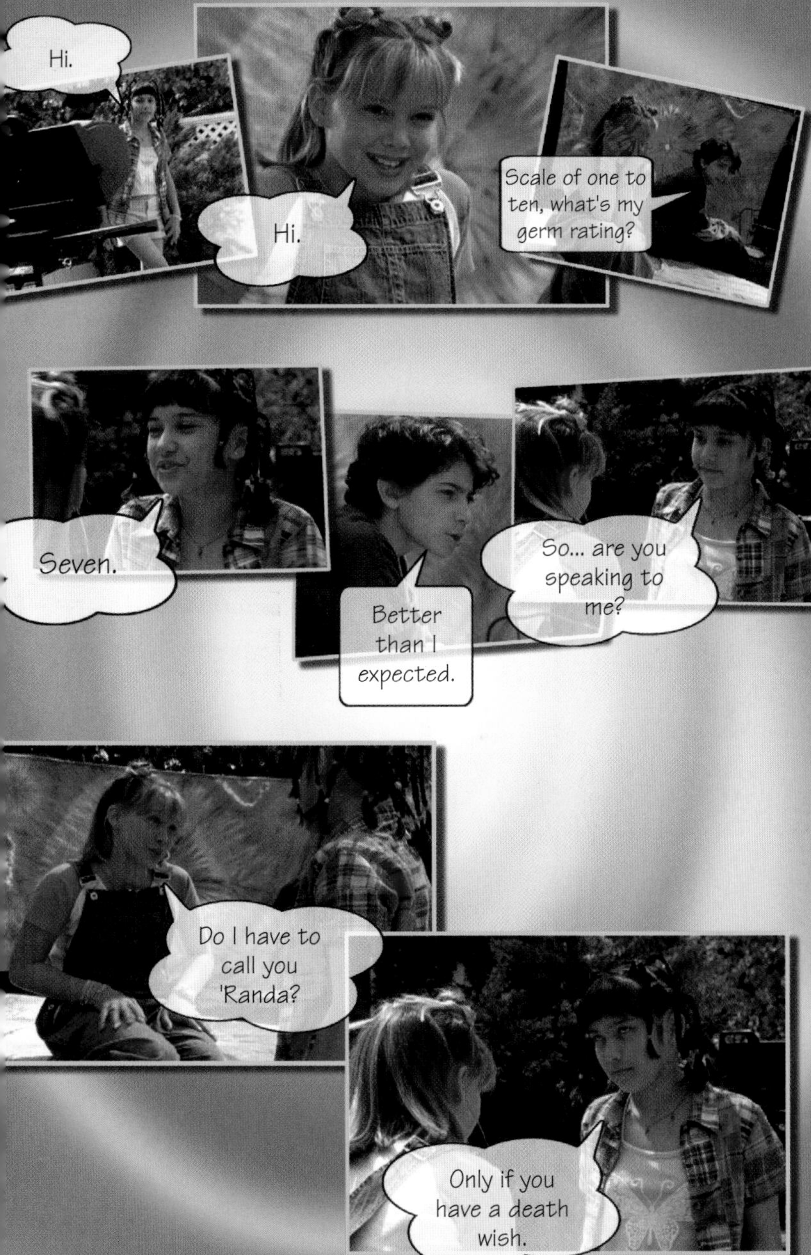
Hi.
Hi.
Scale of one to ten, what's my germ rating?
Seven.
Better than I expected.
So... are you speaking to me?
Do I have to call you 'Randa?
Only if you have a death wish.

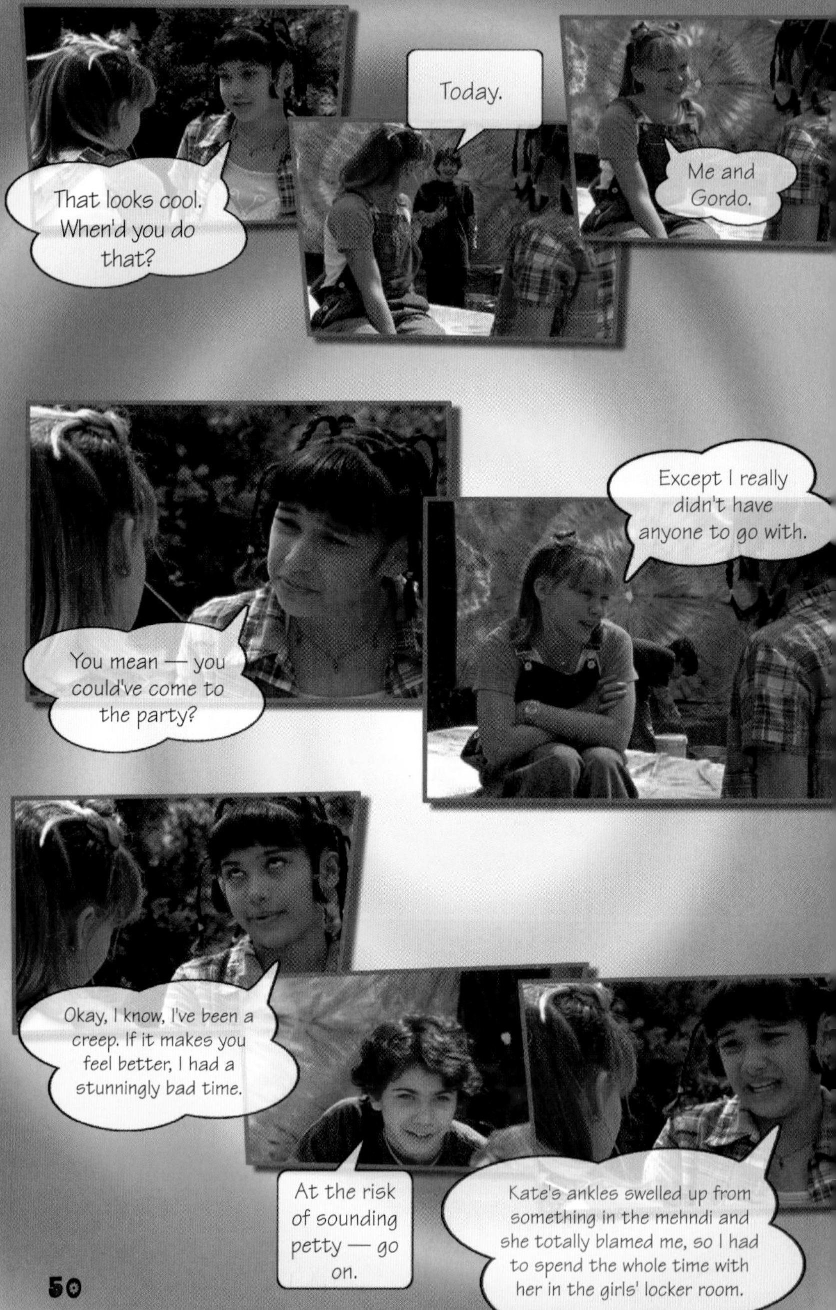
That looks cool. When'd you do that?
Today.
Me and Gordo.
You mean — you could've come to the party?
Except I really didn't have anyone to go with.
Okay, I know, I've been a creep. If it makes you feel better, I had a stunningly bad time.
At the risk of sounding petty — go on.
Kate's ankles swelled up from something in the mehndi and she totally blamed me, so I had to spend the whole time with her in the girls' locker room.

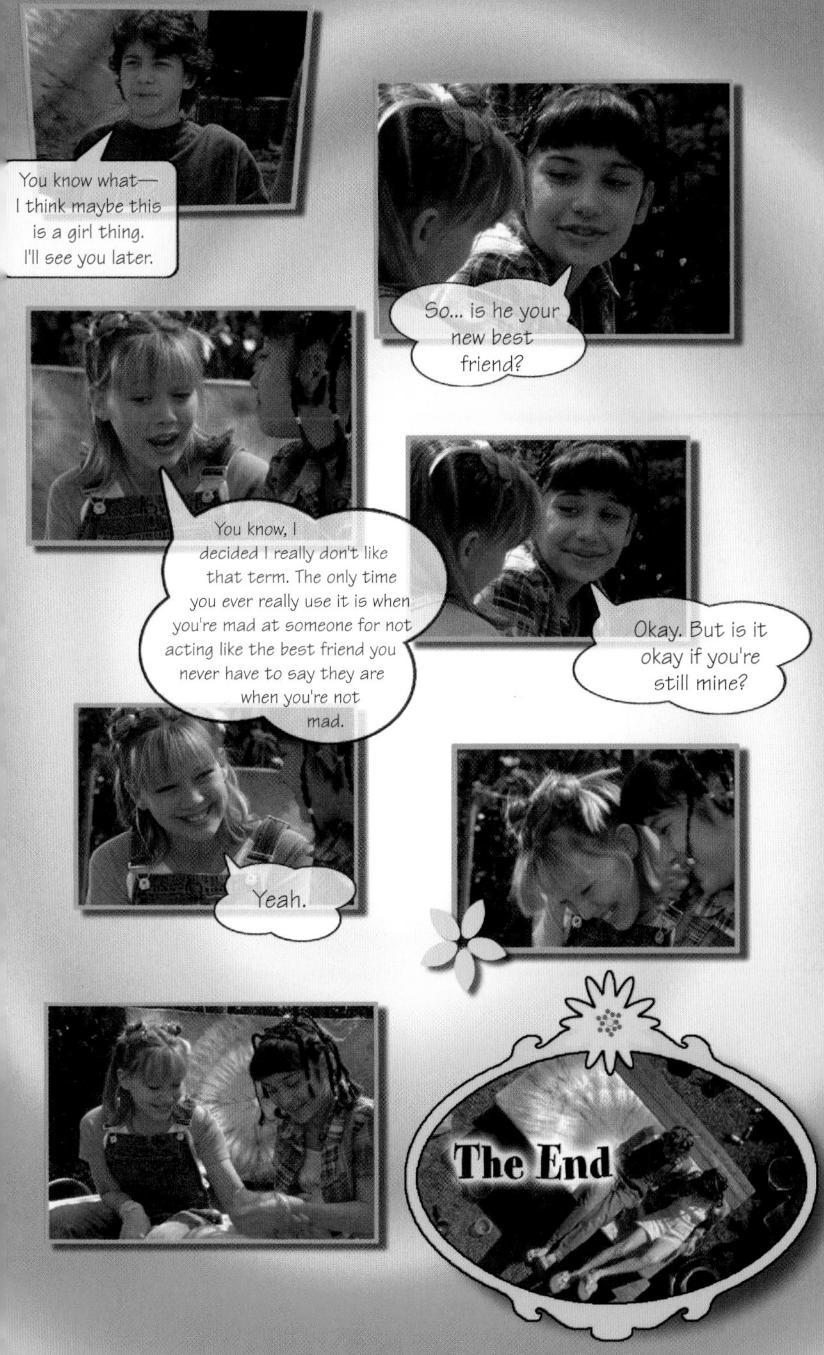

You know what— I think maybe this is a girl thing. I'll see you later.
So... is he your new best friend?
You know, I decided I really don't like that term. The only time you ever really use it is when you're mad at someone for not acting like the best friend you never have to say they are when you're not mad.
Okay. But is it okay if you're still mine?
Yeah.
The End

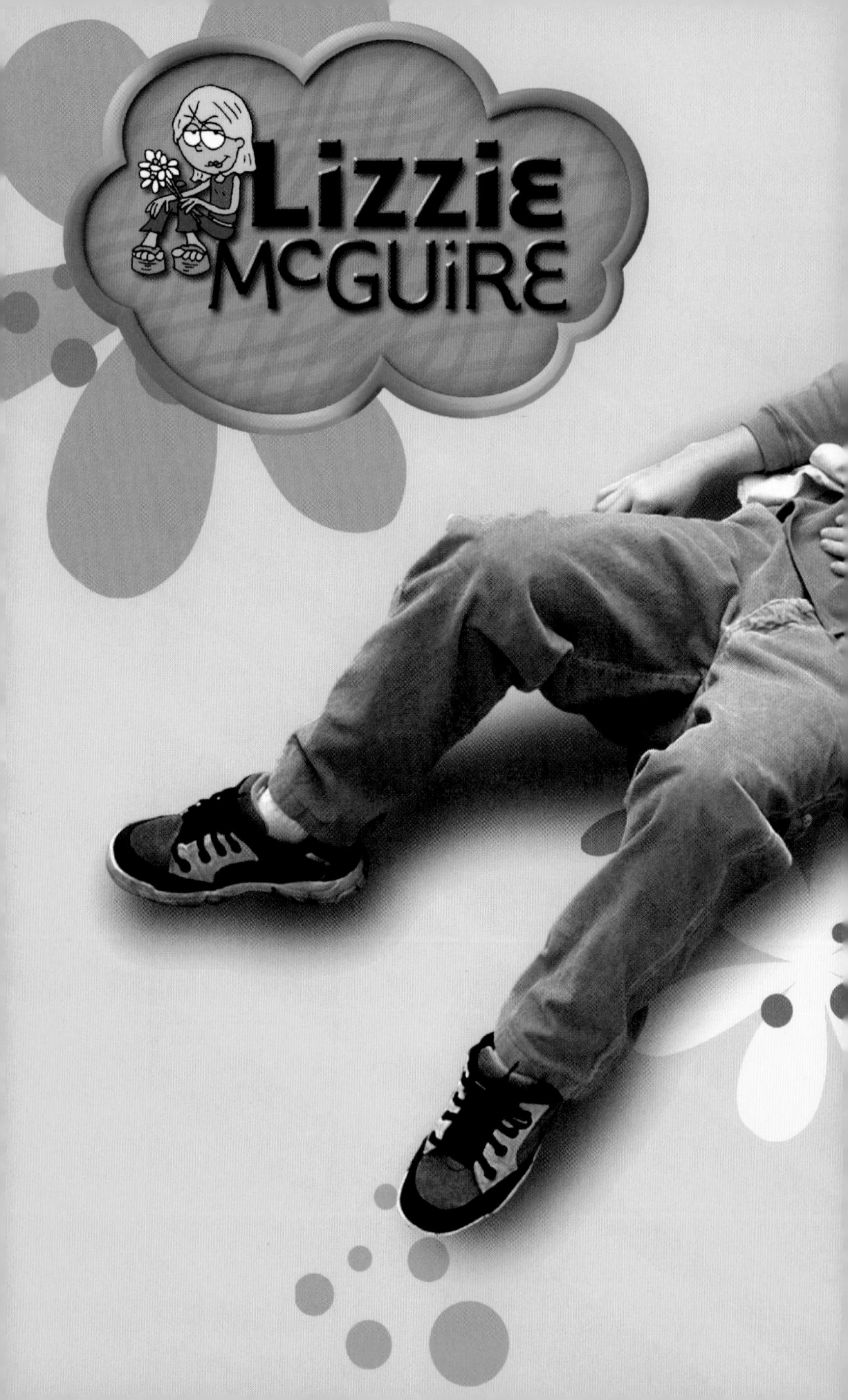
Lizzie
McGuire

Episode 2

"Picture Day"

Lizzie is obsessed with finding just the right outfit for picture day at school, but her moment of glory turns to humiliation when her parents step in and force her to wear a gift from her grandma — a hideous sweater with a cartoon unicorn on it. (Gulp!)

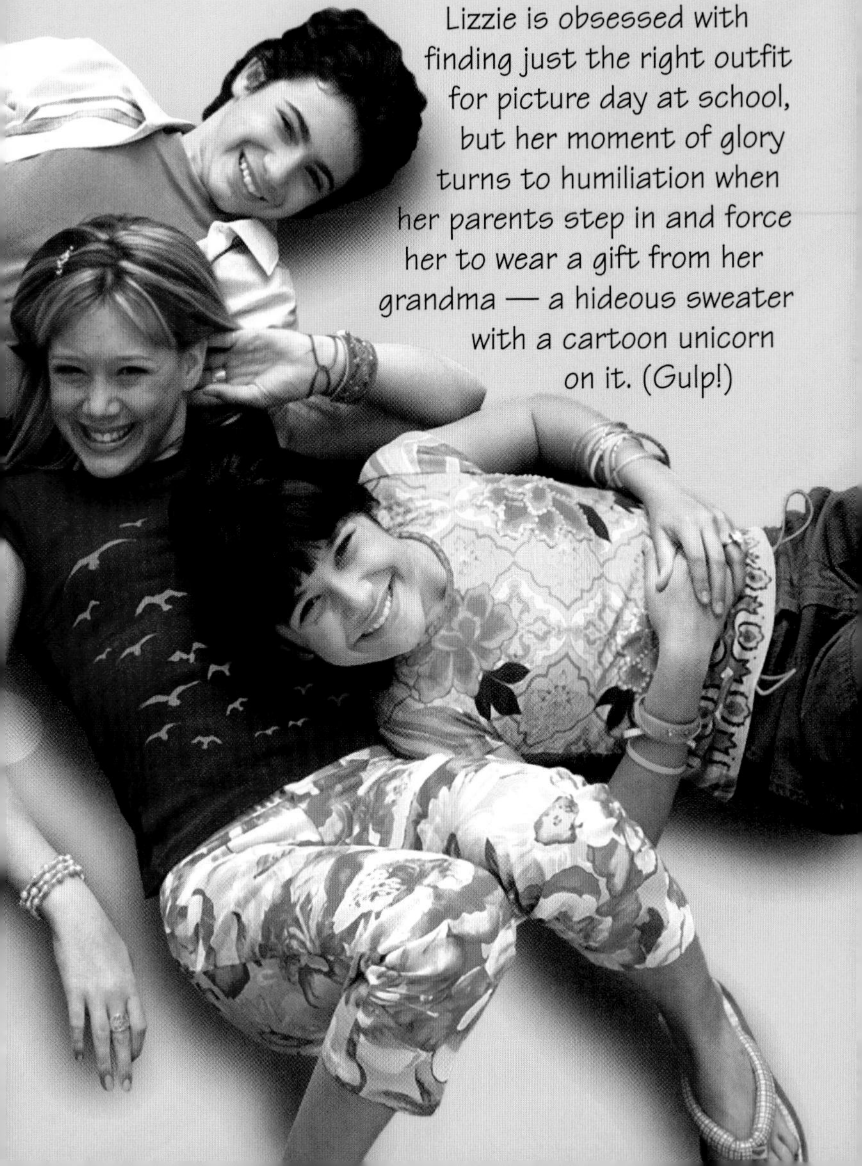

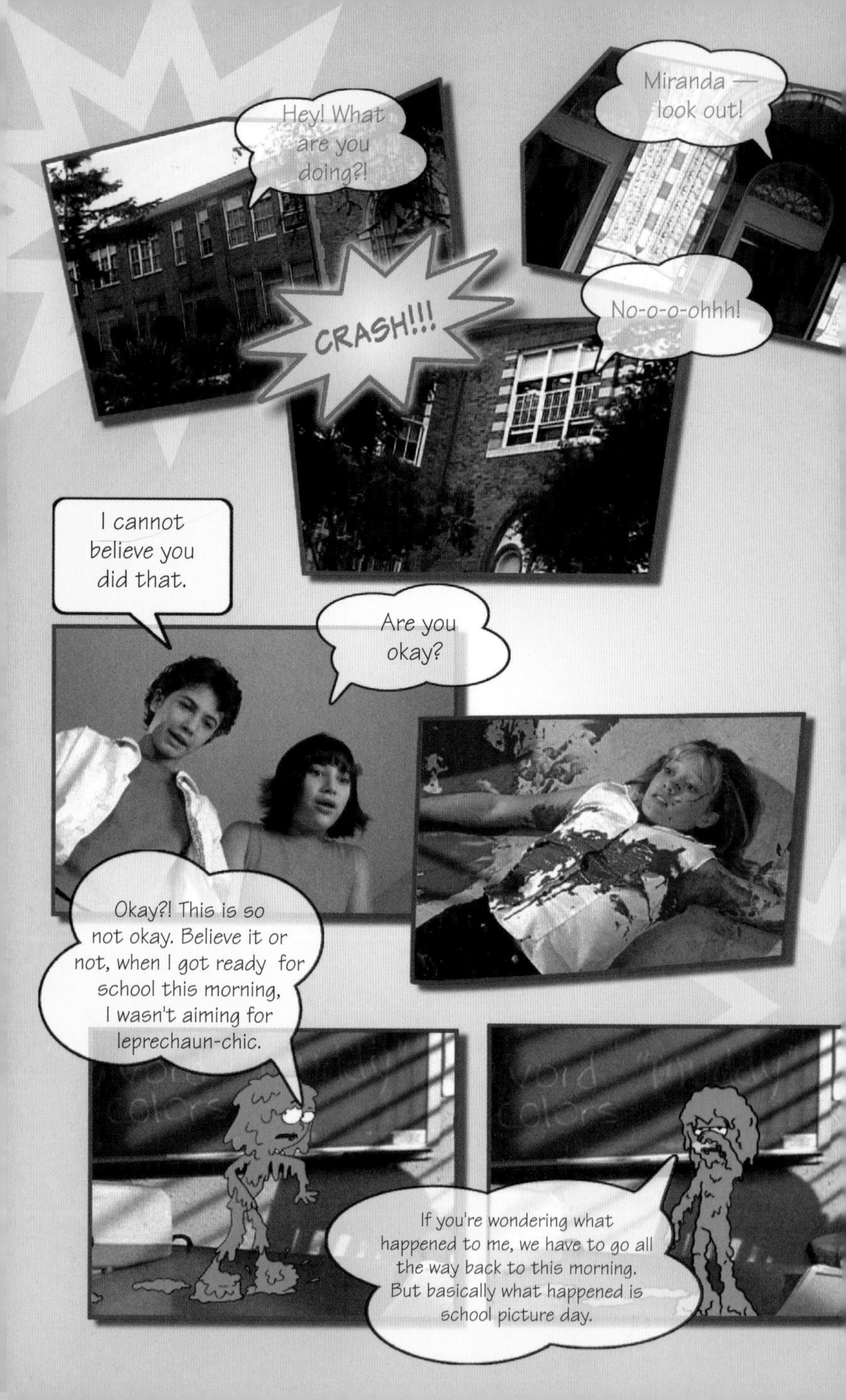
Hey! What are you doing?!
Miranda — look out!
CRASH!!!
No-o-o-ohhh!
I cannot believe you did that.
Are you okay?
Okay?! This is so not okay. Believe it or not, when I got ready for school this morning, I wasn't aiming for leprechaun-chic.
If you're wondering what happened to me, we have to go all the way back to this morning. But basically what happened is school picture day.

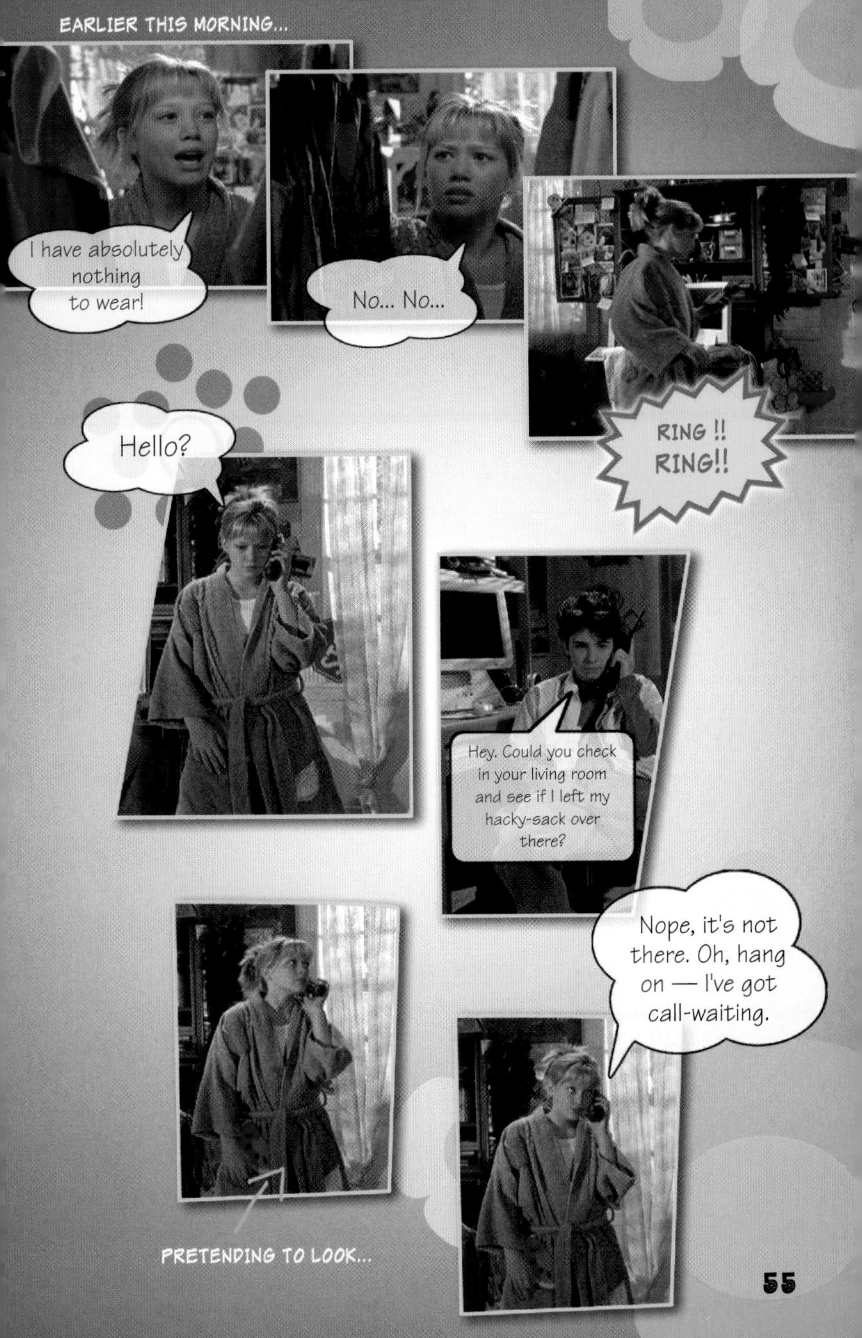
EARLIER THIS MORNING...
I have absolutely nothing to wear!
No... No...
RING !! RING!!
Hello?
Hey. Could you check in your living room and see if I left my hacky-sack over there?
Nope, it's not there. Oh, hang on — I've got call-waiting.
PRETENDING TO LOOK...

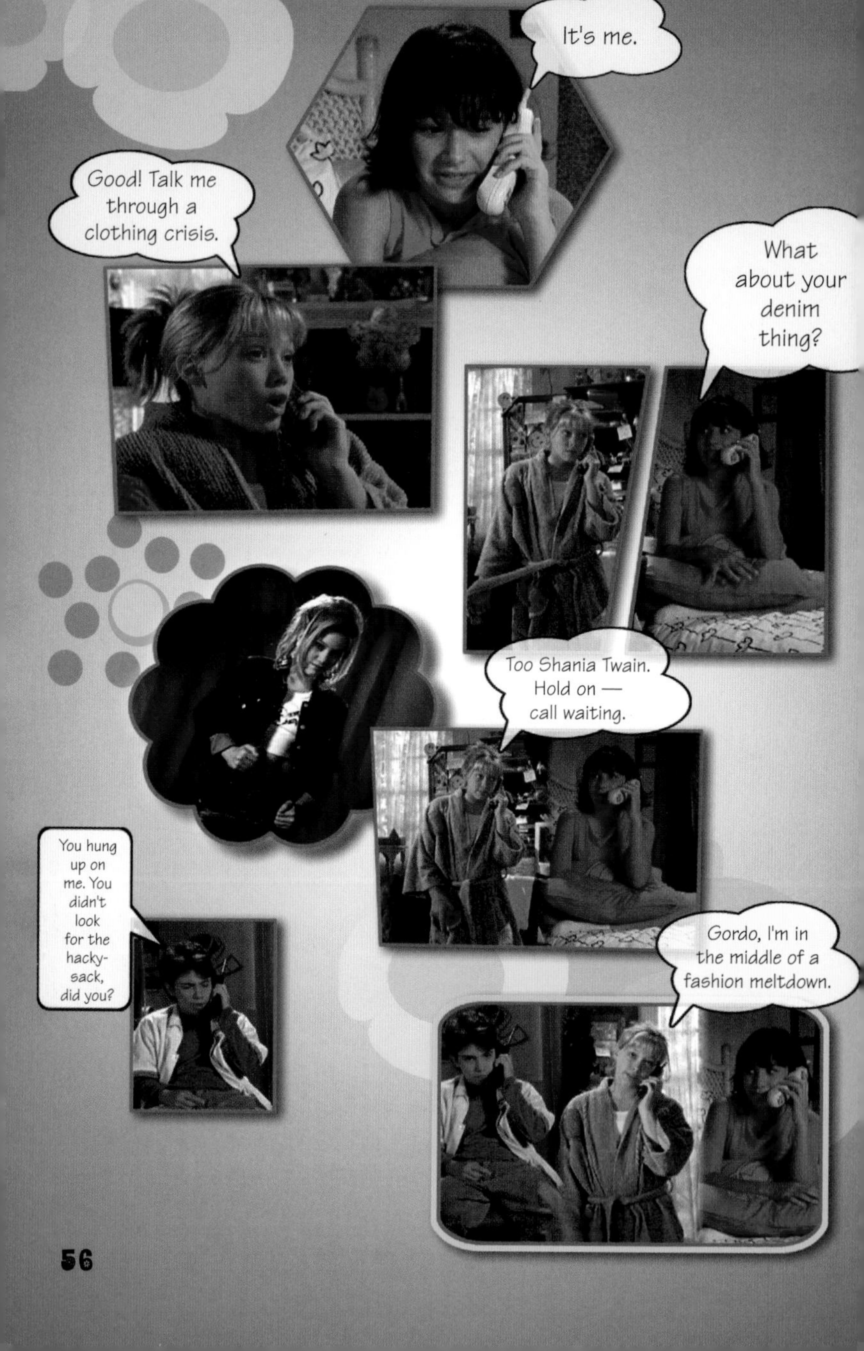
It's me.
Good! Talk me through a clothing crisis.
What about your denim thing?
Too Shania Twain. Hold on — call waiting.
You hung up on me. You didn't look for the hacky-sack, did you?
Gordo, I'm in the middle of a fashion meltdown.

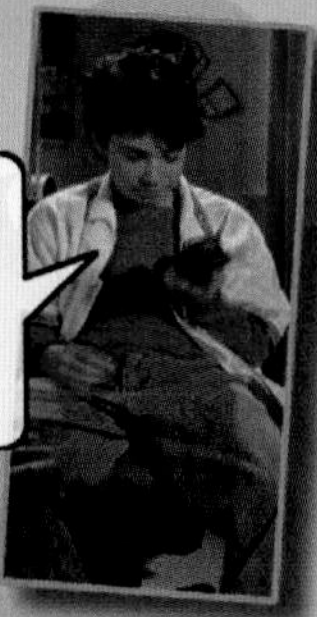
All righty, then. Chicks...

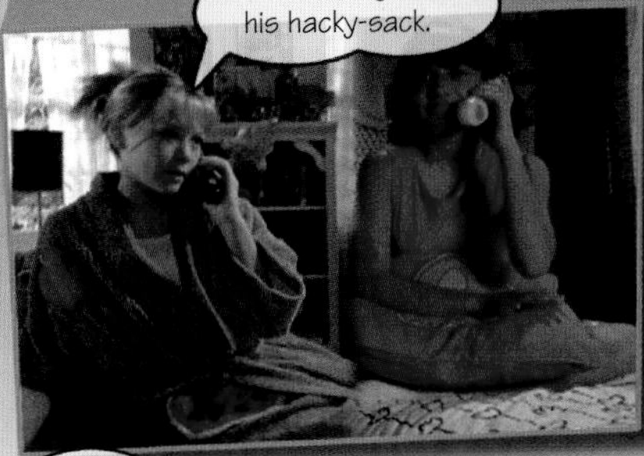
That was Gordo. He's obsessing about his hacky-sack.

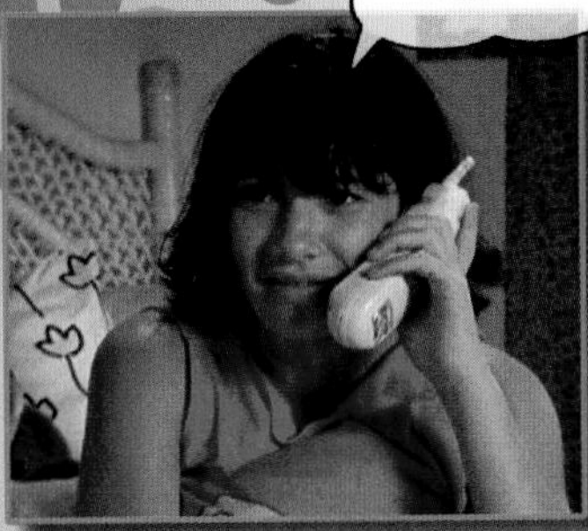
Boys...

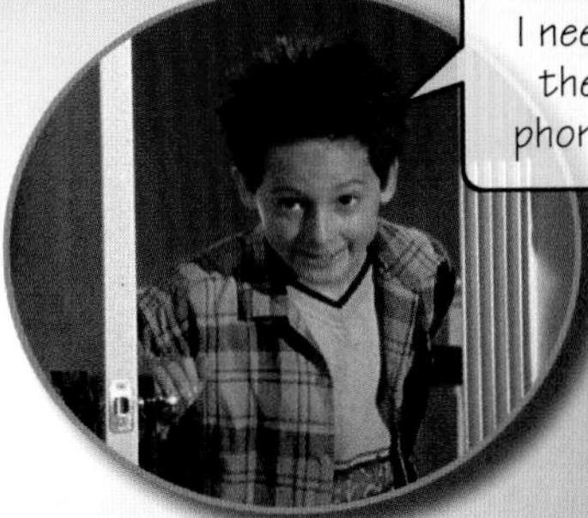
Lizzie, I need the phone.

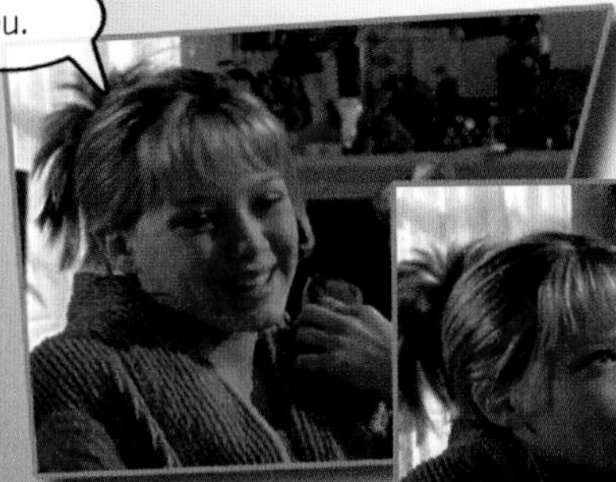
Well, that's a big problem for you.

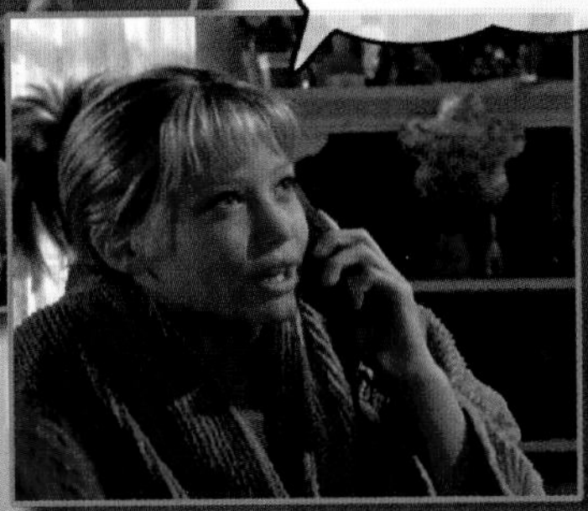
You're so lucky you've got that Delia's outfit.

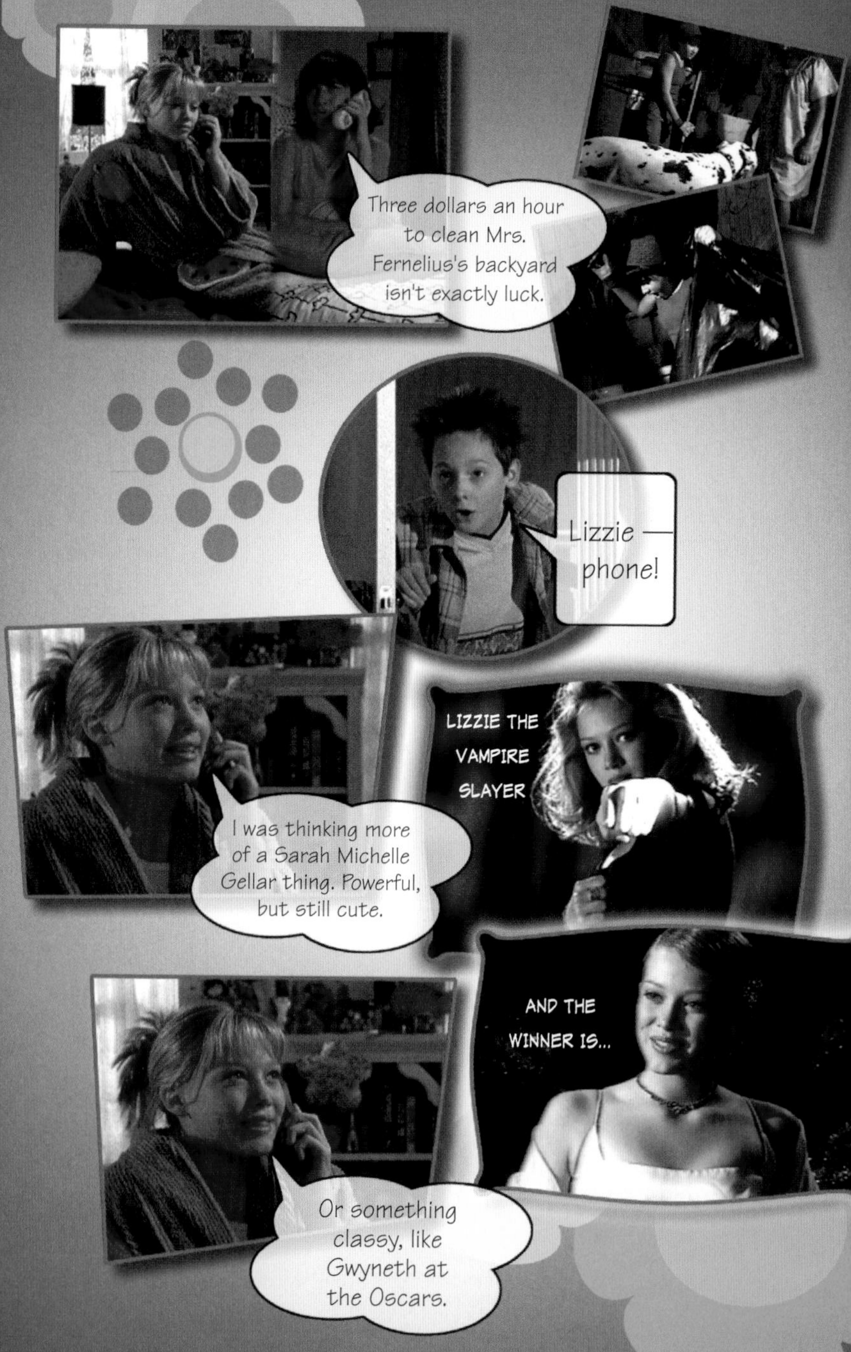
Three dollars an hour to clean Mrs. Fernelius's backyard isn't exactly luck.
Lizzie — phone!
I was thinking more of a Sarah Michelle Gellar thing. Powerful, but still cute.
LIZZIE THE VAMPIRE SLAYER
Or something classy, like Gwyneth at the Oscars.
AND THE WINNER IS...

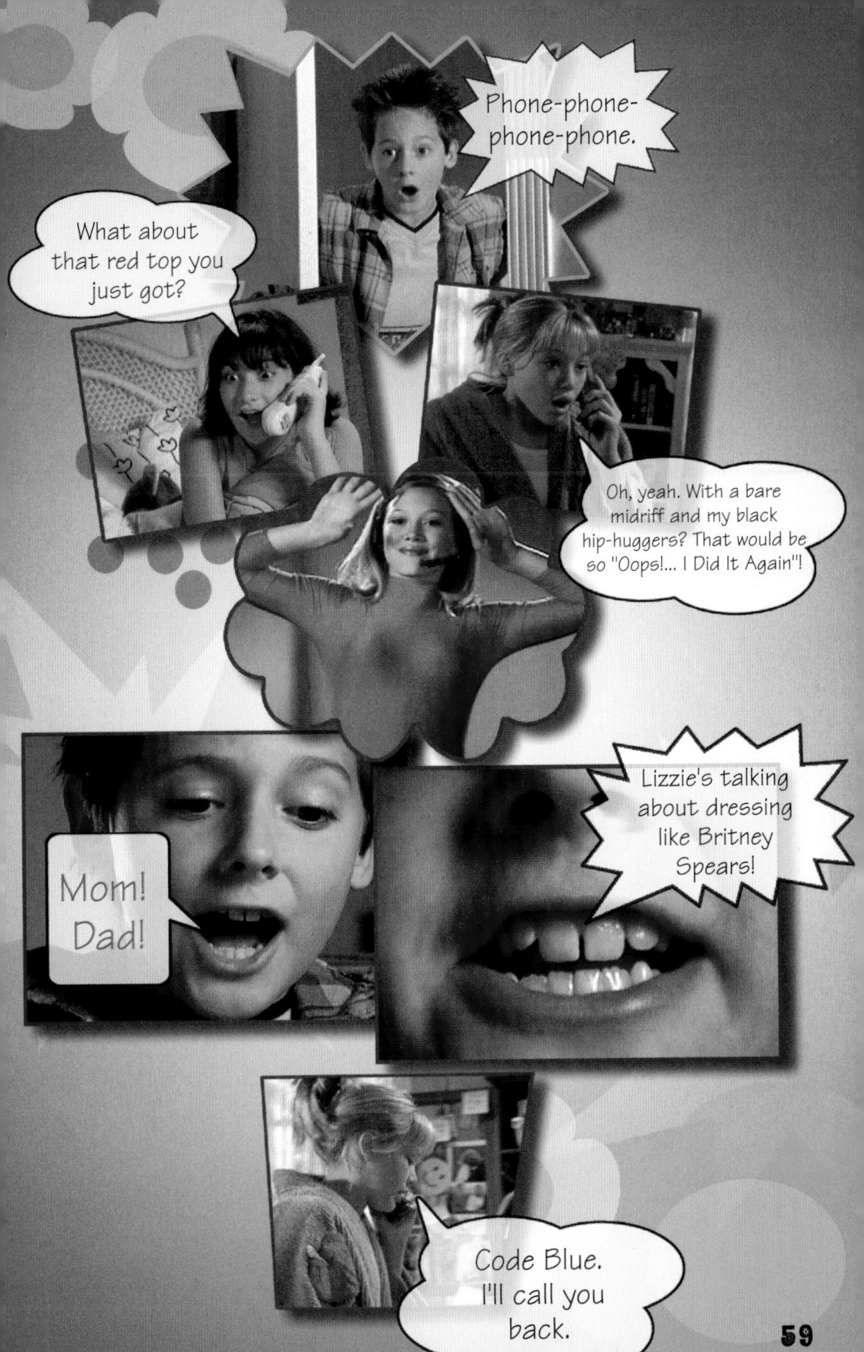
Phone-phone-phone-phone.
What about that red top you just got?
Oh, yeah. With a bare midriff and my black hip-huggers? That would be so "Oops!... I Did It Again"!
Mom! Dad!
Lizzie's talking about dressing like Britney Spears!
Code Blue. I'll call you back.

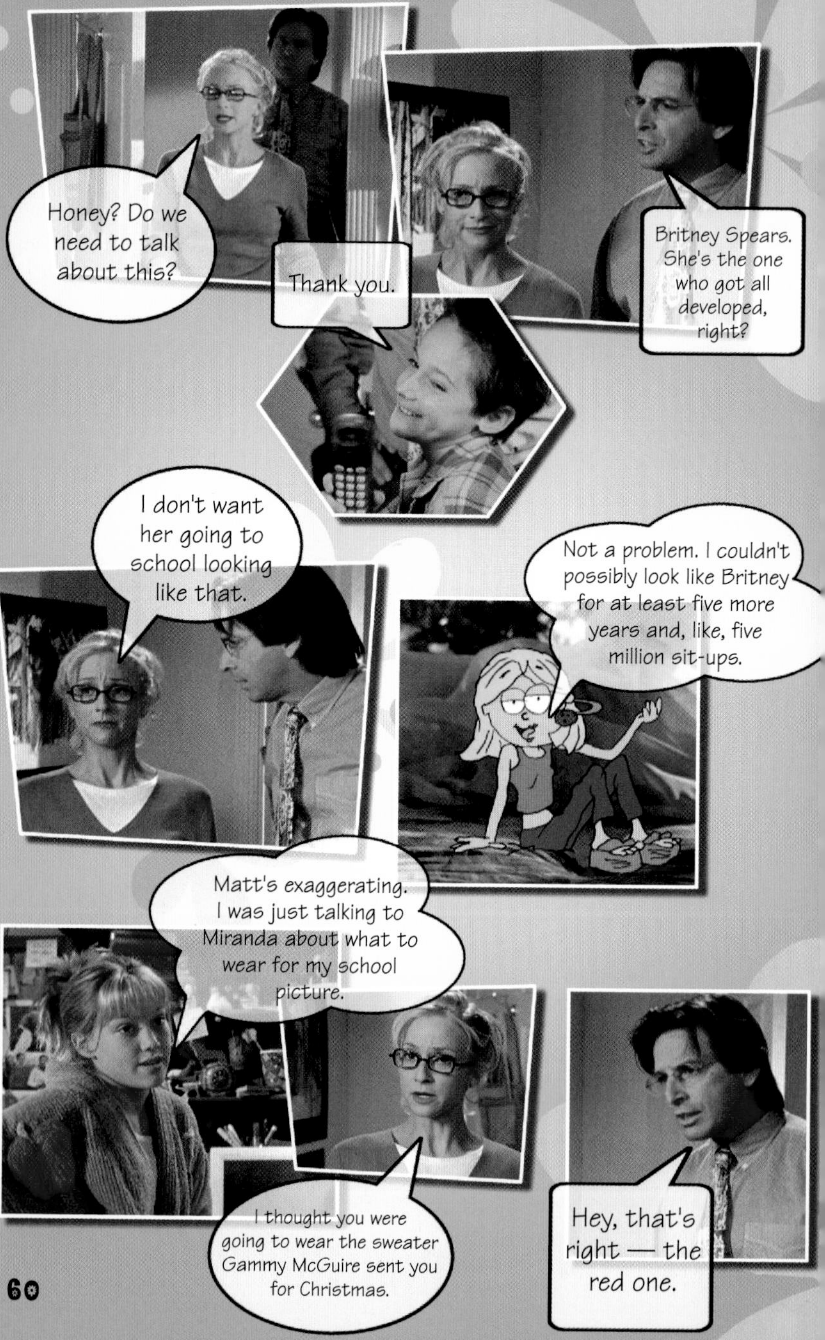
Honey? Do we need to talk about this?
Britney Spears. She's the one who got all developed, right?
Thank you.
I don't want her going to school looking like that.
Not a problem. I couldn't possibly look like Britney for at least five more years and, like, five million sit-ups.
Matt's exaggerating. I was just talking to Miranda about what to wear for my school picture.
I thought you were going to wear the sweater Gammy McGuire sent you for Christmas.
Hey, that's right — the red one.

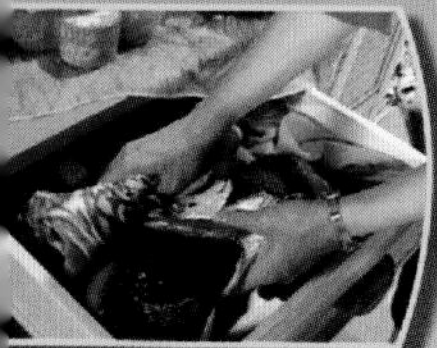

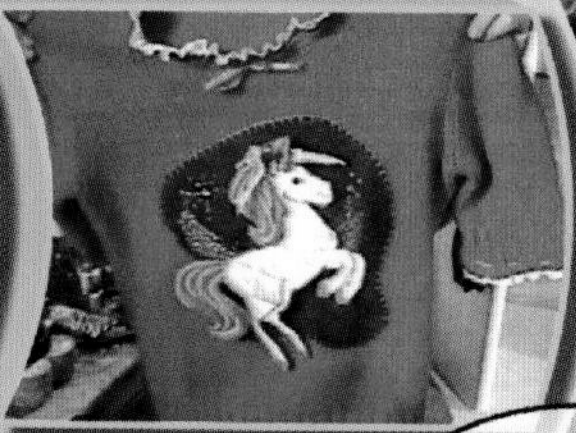

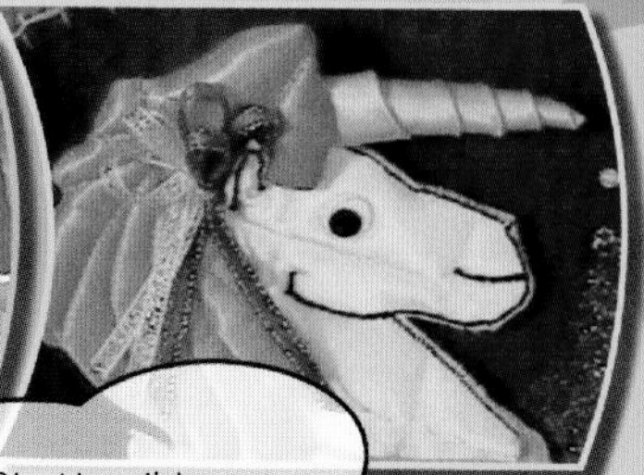

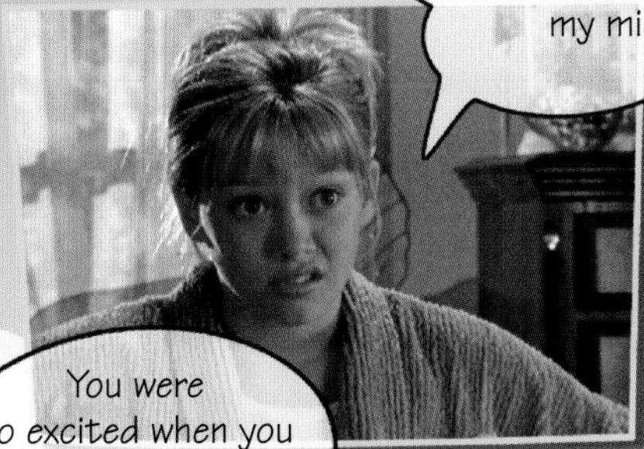
Oh. Um, I'd sort of changed my mind.

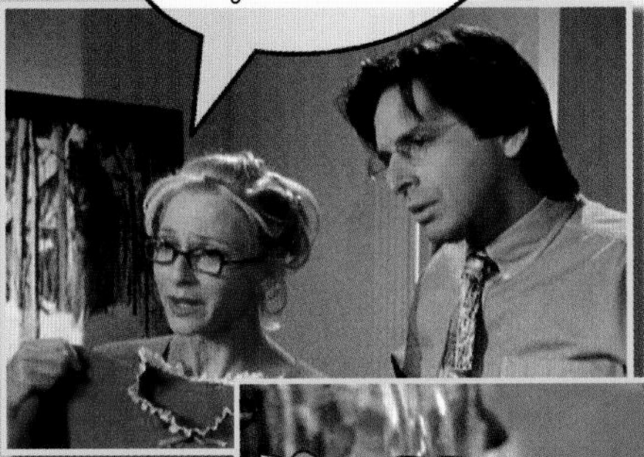
You were so excited when you got it. Why wouldn't you wear it?

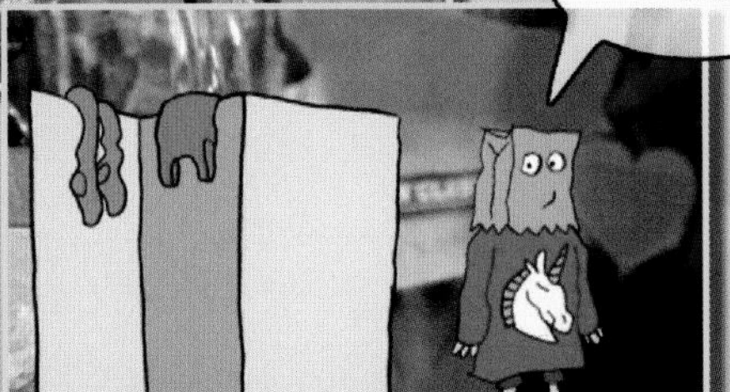
Maybe because it's hideous and makes me look like a cookie-elf.

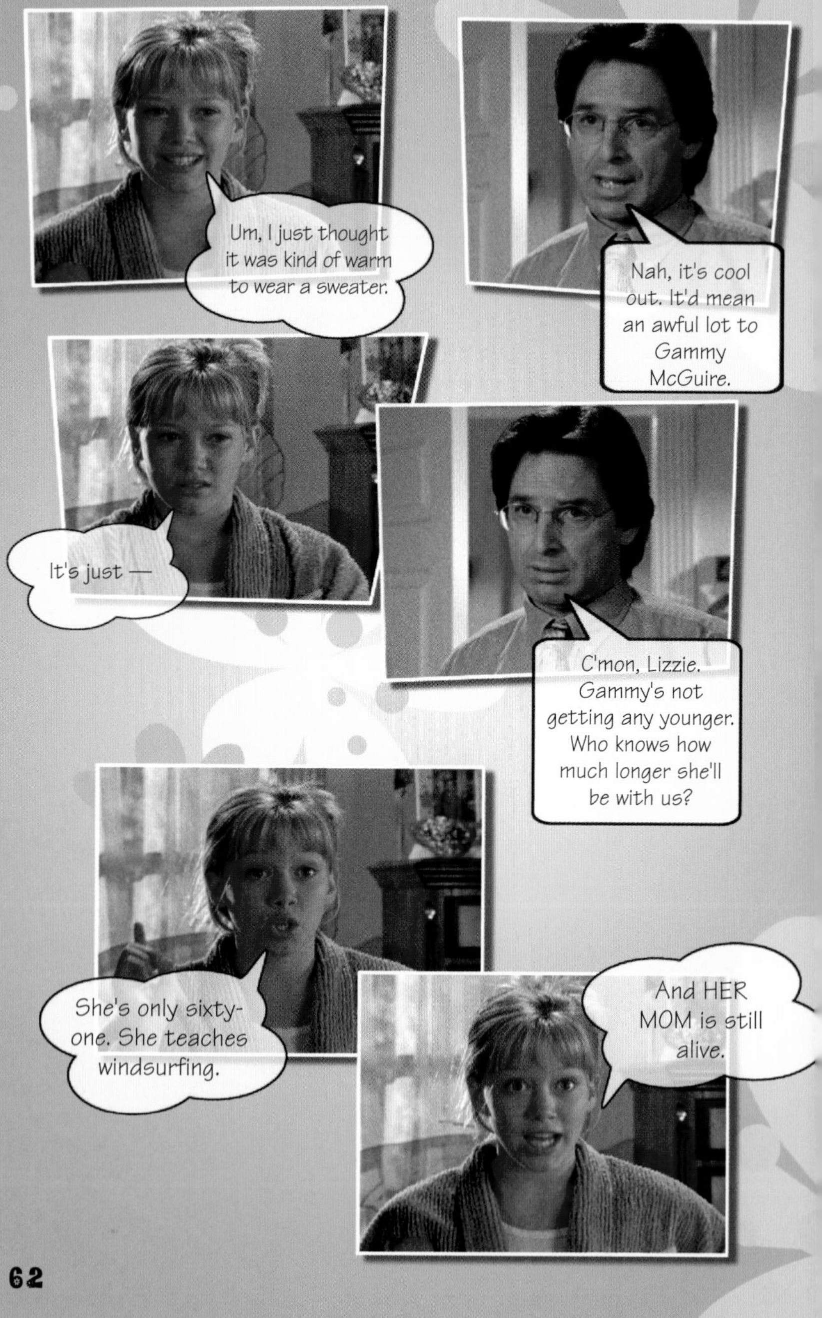
Um, I just thought it was kind of warm to wear a sweater.
Nah, it's cool out. It'd mean an awful lot to Gammy McGuire.
It's just —
C'mon, Lizzie. Gammy's not getting any younger. Who knows how much longer she'll be with us?
She's only sixty-one. She teaches windsurfing.
And HER MOM is still alive.

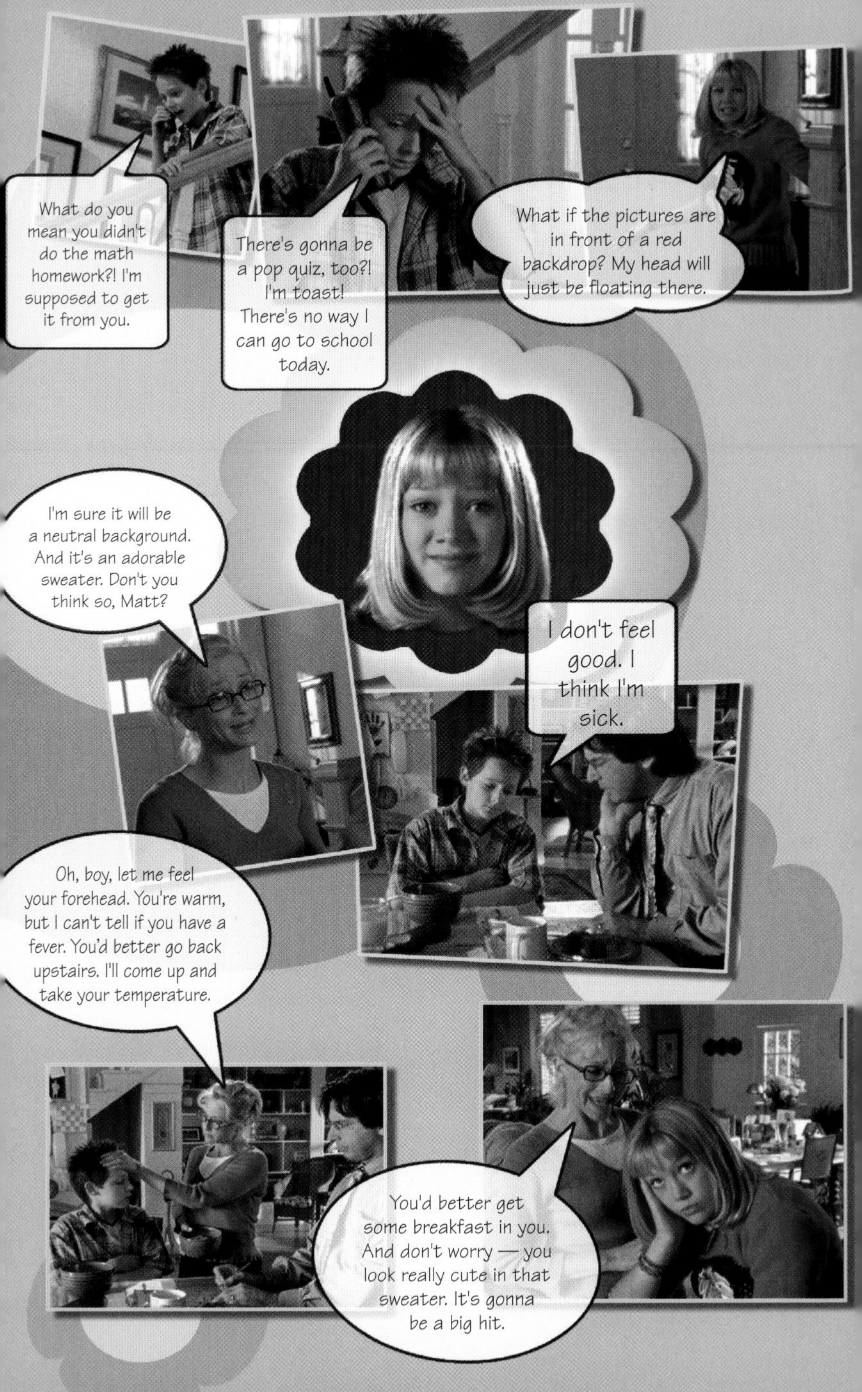
What do you mean you didn't do the math homework?! I'm supposed to get it from you.
There's gonna be a pop quiz, too?! I'm toast! There's no way I can go to school today.
What if the pictures are in front of a red backdrop? My head will just be floating there.
I'm sure it will be a neutral background. And it's an adorable sweater. Don't you think so, Matt?
I don't feel good. I think I'm sick.
Oh, boy, let me feel your forehead. You're warm, but I can't tell if you have a fever. You'd better go back upstairs. I'll come up and take your temperature.
You'd better get some breakfast in you. And don't worry — you look really cute in that sweater. It's gonna be a big hit.

WALKING TO THE BUS STOP...

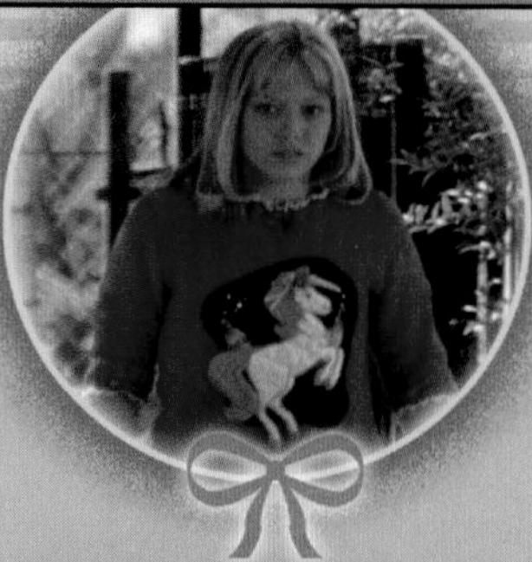

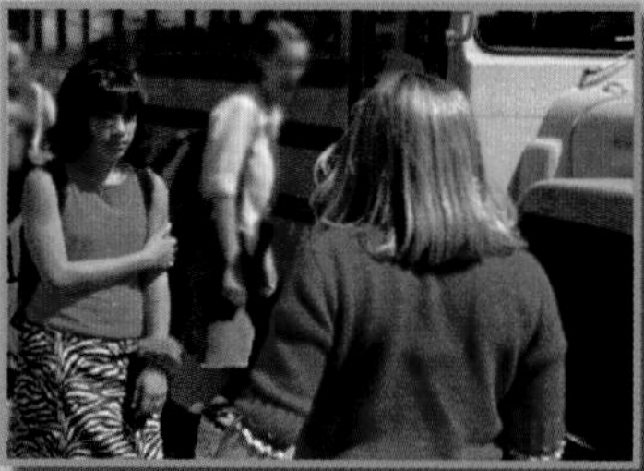

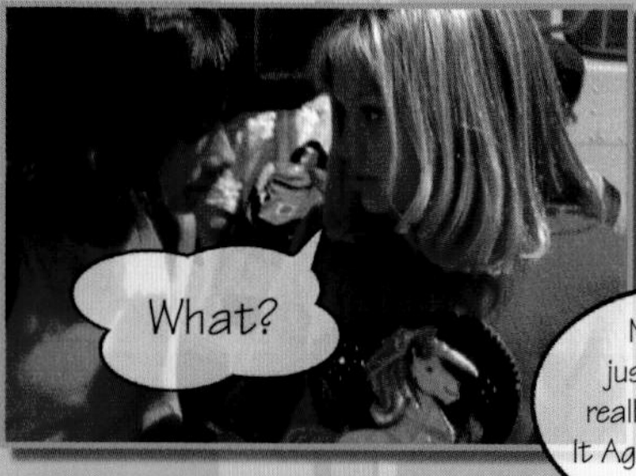
What?

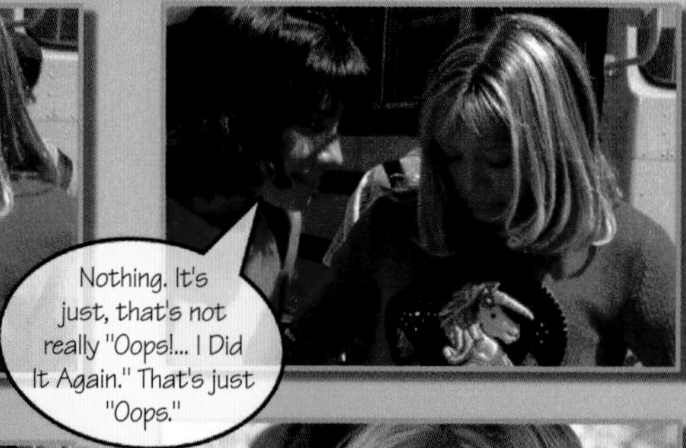
Nothing. It's just, that's not really "Oops!... I Did It Again." That's just "Oops."

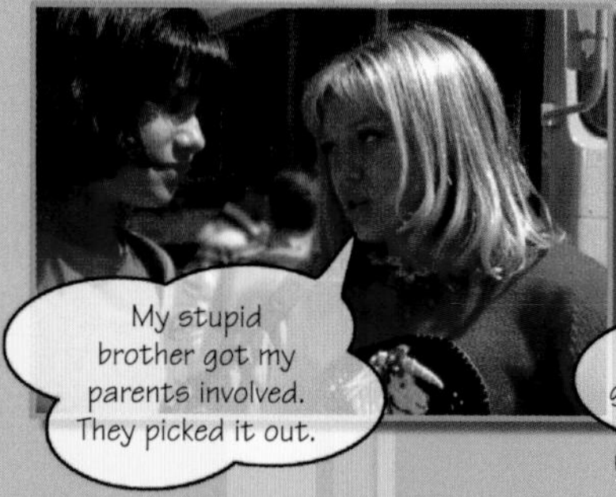
My stupid brother got my parents involved. They picked it out.

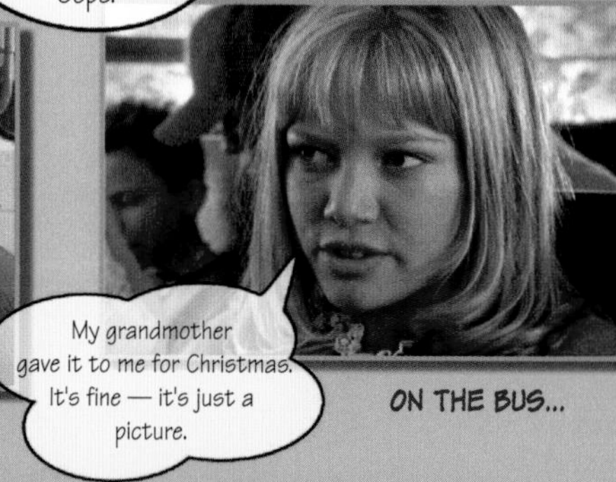
My grandmother gave it to me for Christmas. It's fine — it's just a picture.

ON THE BUS...

It is not just a picture. We're in middle school now — these pictures don't just go home in an envelope, they get published in the yearbook.

This is serious. This picture will be seen by everybody, forever.

Forever?

Forever. I mean, haven't you seen your parents' yearbook pictures?

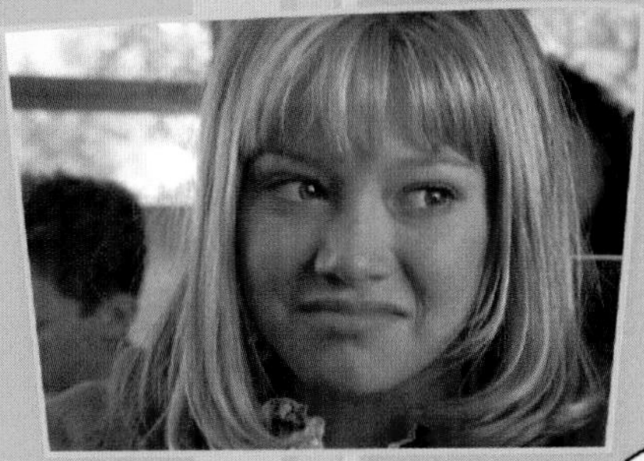

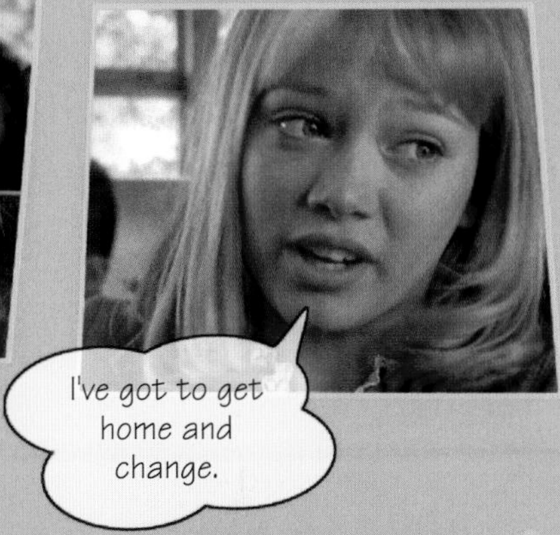
I've got to get home and change.

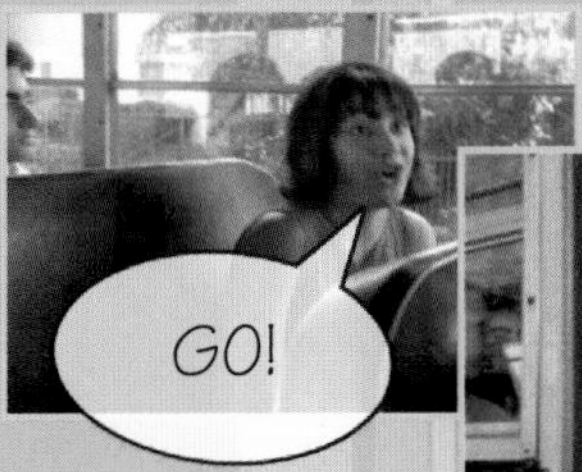
GO!

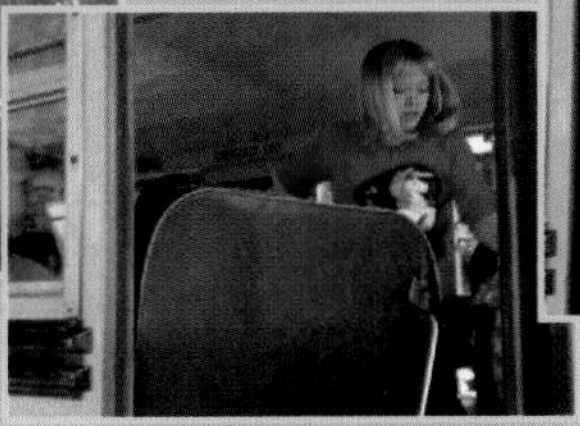

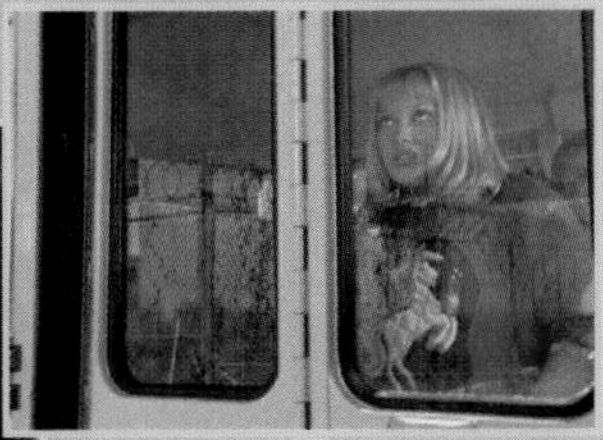

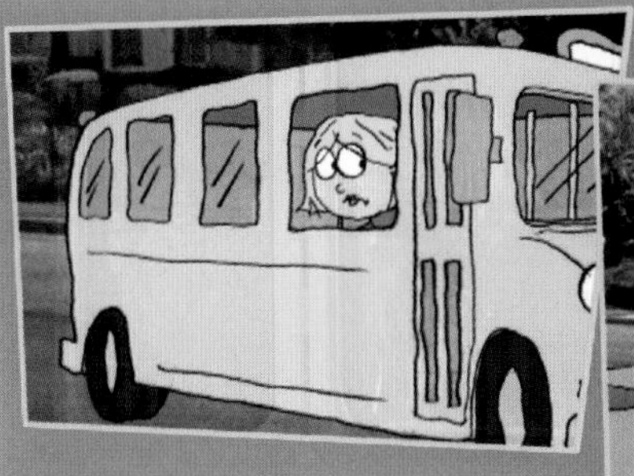

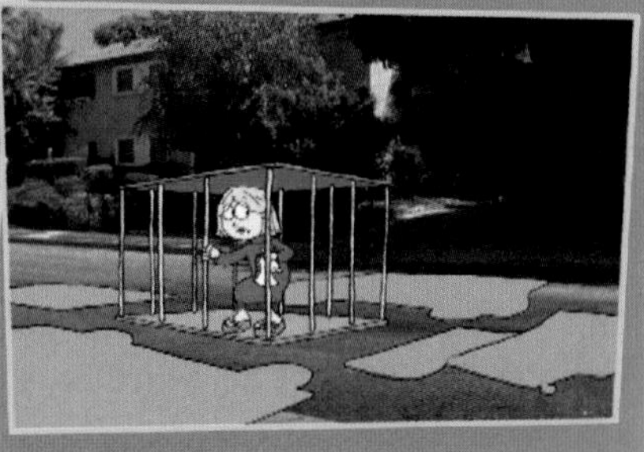

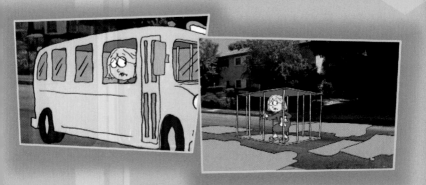

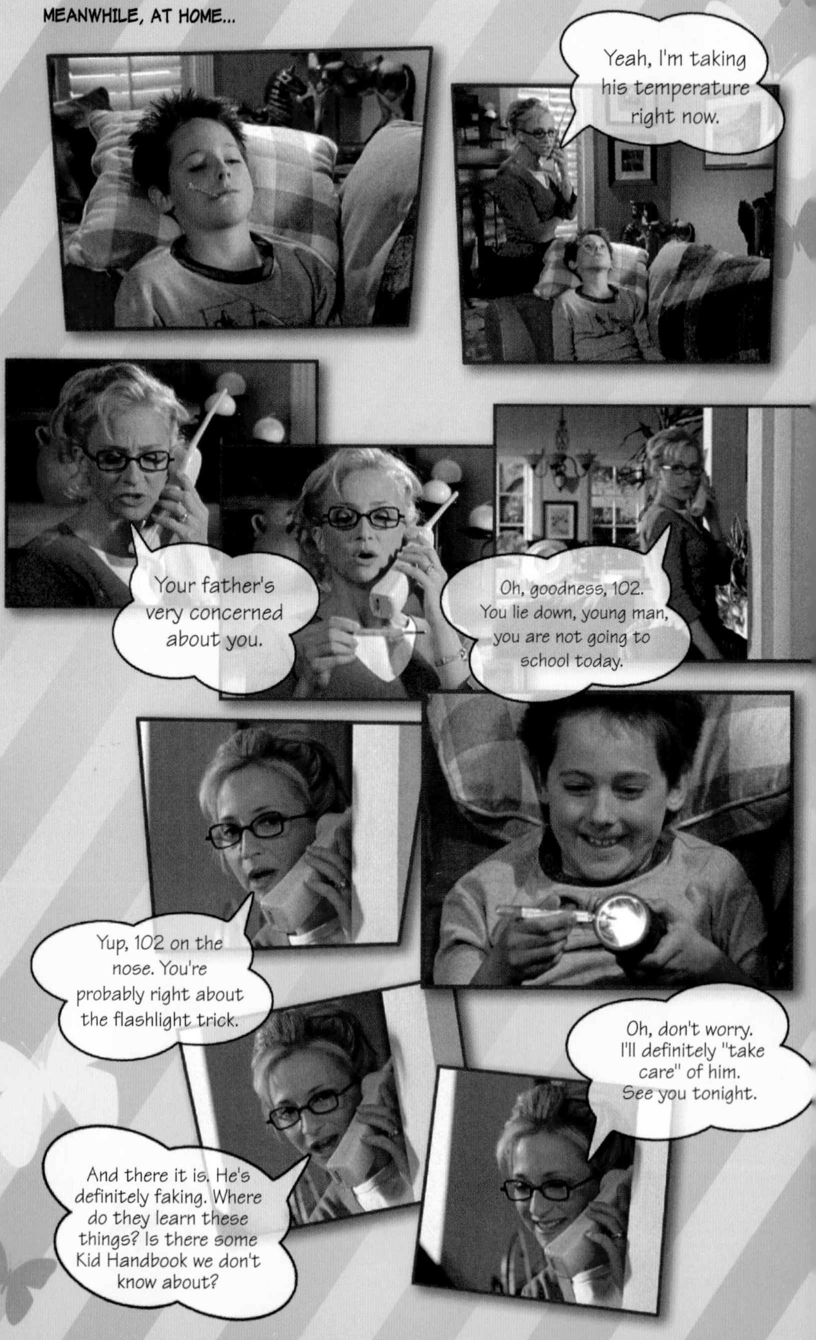
MEANWHILE, AT HOME...
Yeah, I'm taking his temperature right now.
Your father's very concerned about you.
Oh, goodness, 102. You lie down, young man, you are not going to school today.
Yup, 102 on the nose. You're probably right about the flashlight trick.
And there it is. He's definitely faking. Where do they learn these things? Is there some Kid Handbook we don't know about?
Oh, don't worry. I'll definitely "take care" of him. See you tonight.

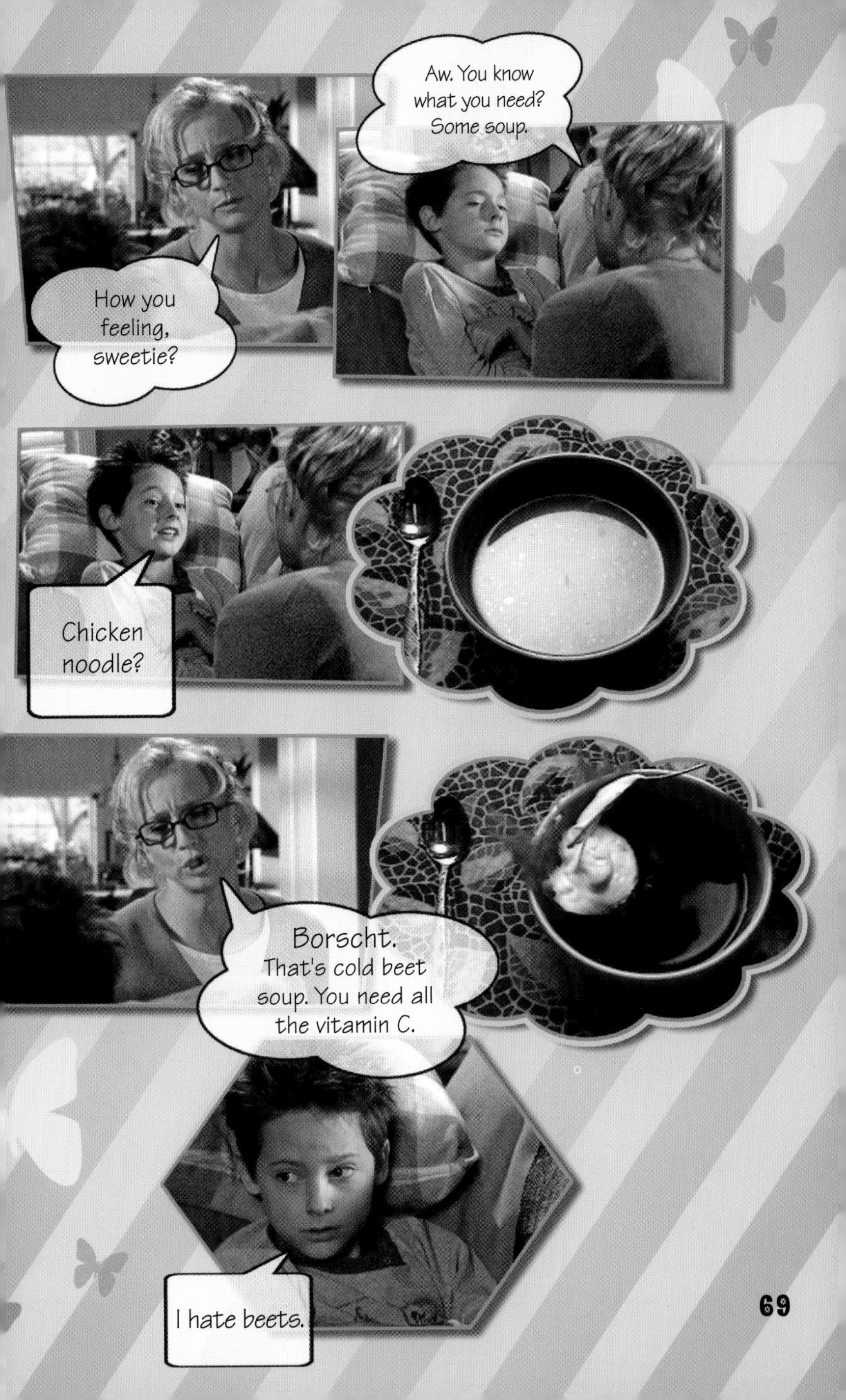
How you feeling, sweetie?
Aw. You know what you need? Some soup.
Chicken noodle?
Borscht. That's cold beet soup. You need all the vitamin C.
I hate beets.

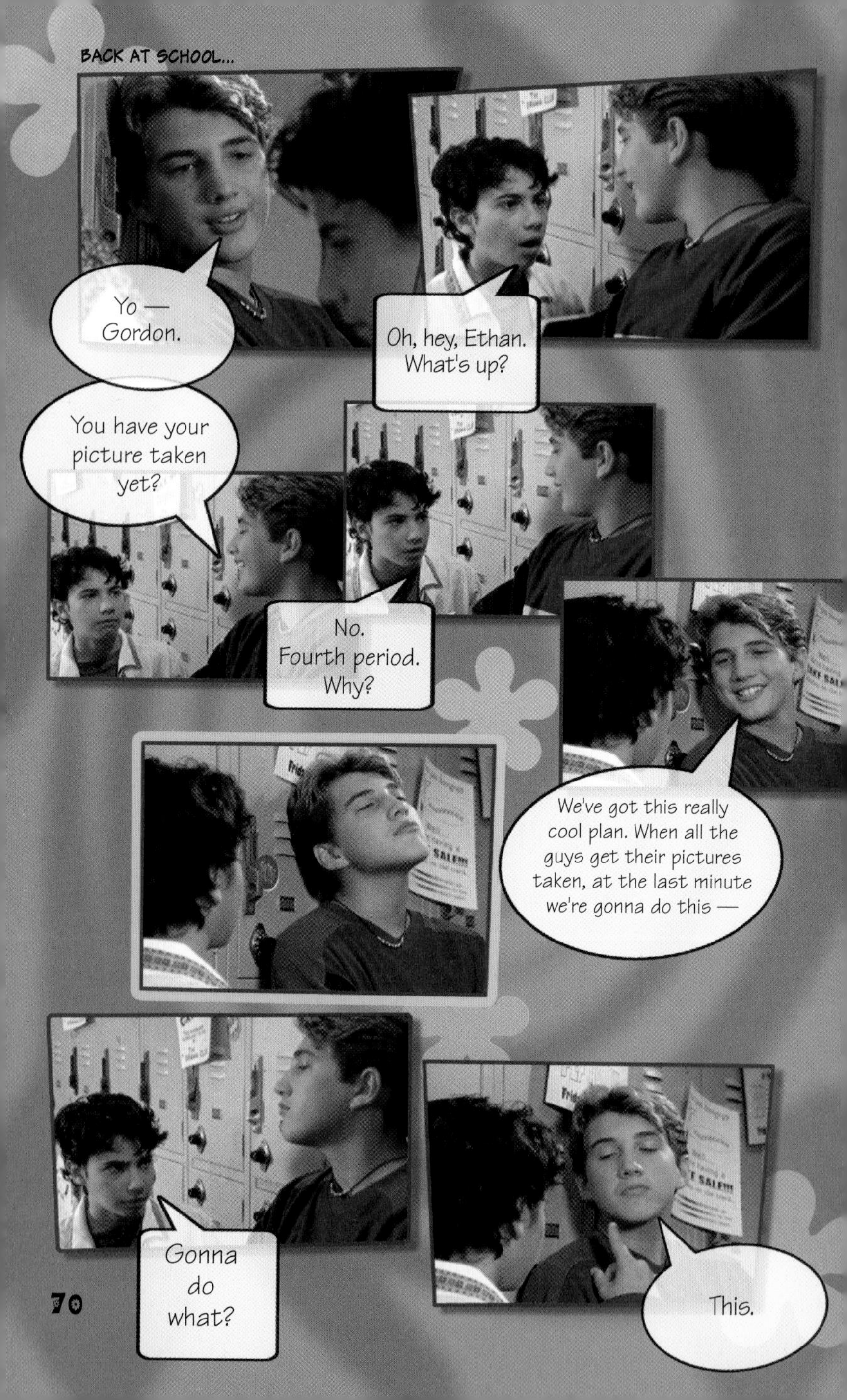
BACK AT SCHOOL...
Yo — Gordon.
Oh, hey, Ethan. What's up?
You have your picture taken yet?
No. Fourth period. Why?
We've got this really cool plan. When all the guys get their pictures taken, at the last minute we're gonna do this —
Gonna do what?
This.

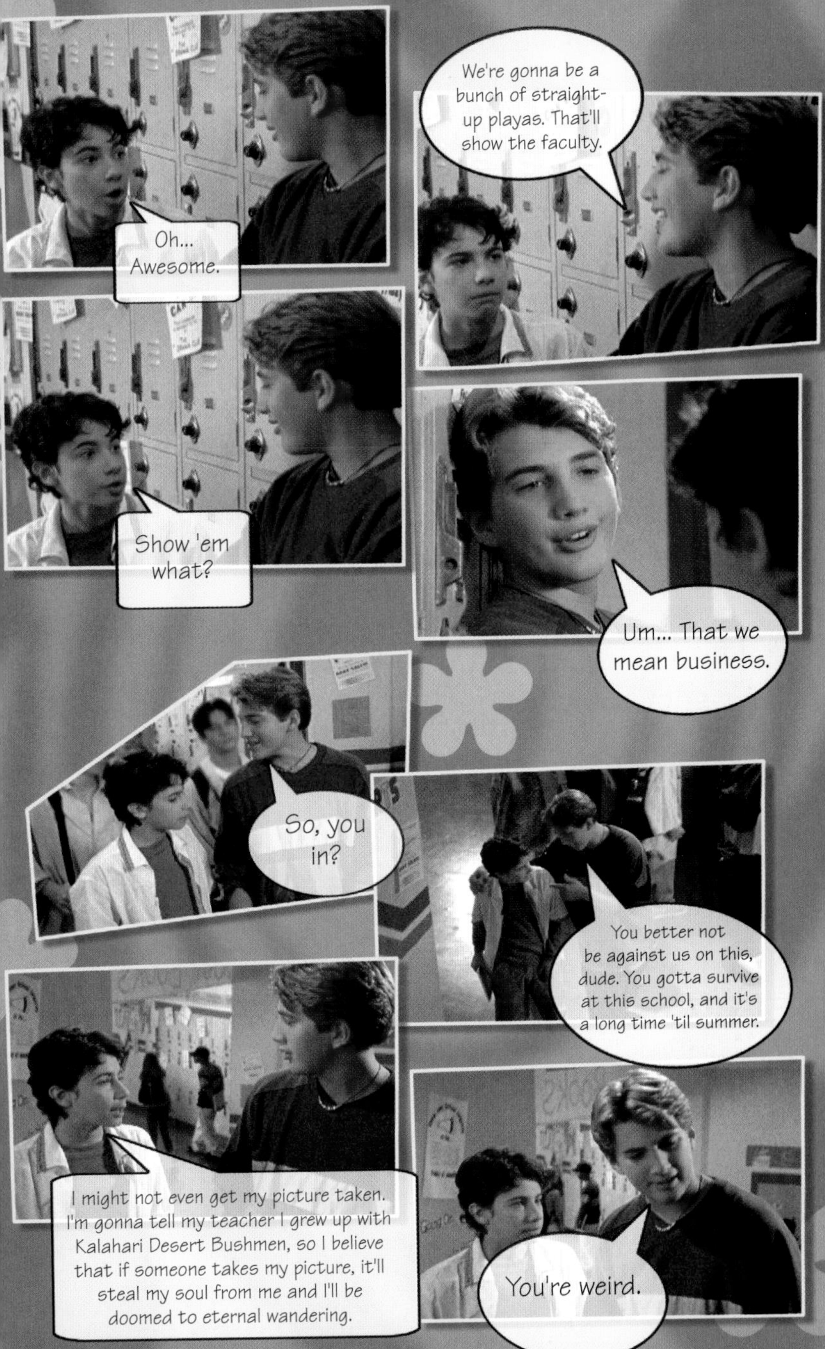
Oh... Awesome.
We're gonna be a bunch of straight-up playas. That'll show the faculty.
Show 'em what?
Um... That we mean business.
So, you in?
You better not be against us on this, dude. You gotta survive at this school, and it's a long time 'til summer.
I might not even get my picture taken. I'm gonna tell my teacher I grew up with Kalahari Desert Bushmen, so I believe that if someone takes my picture, it'll steal my soul from me and I'll be doomed to eternal wandering.
You're weird.

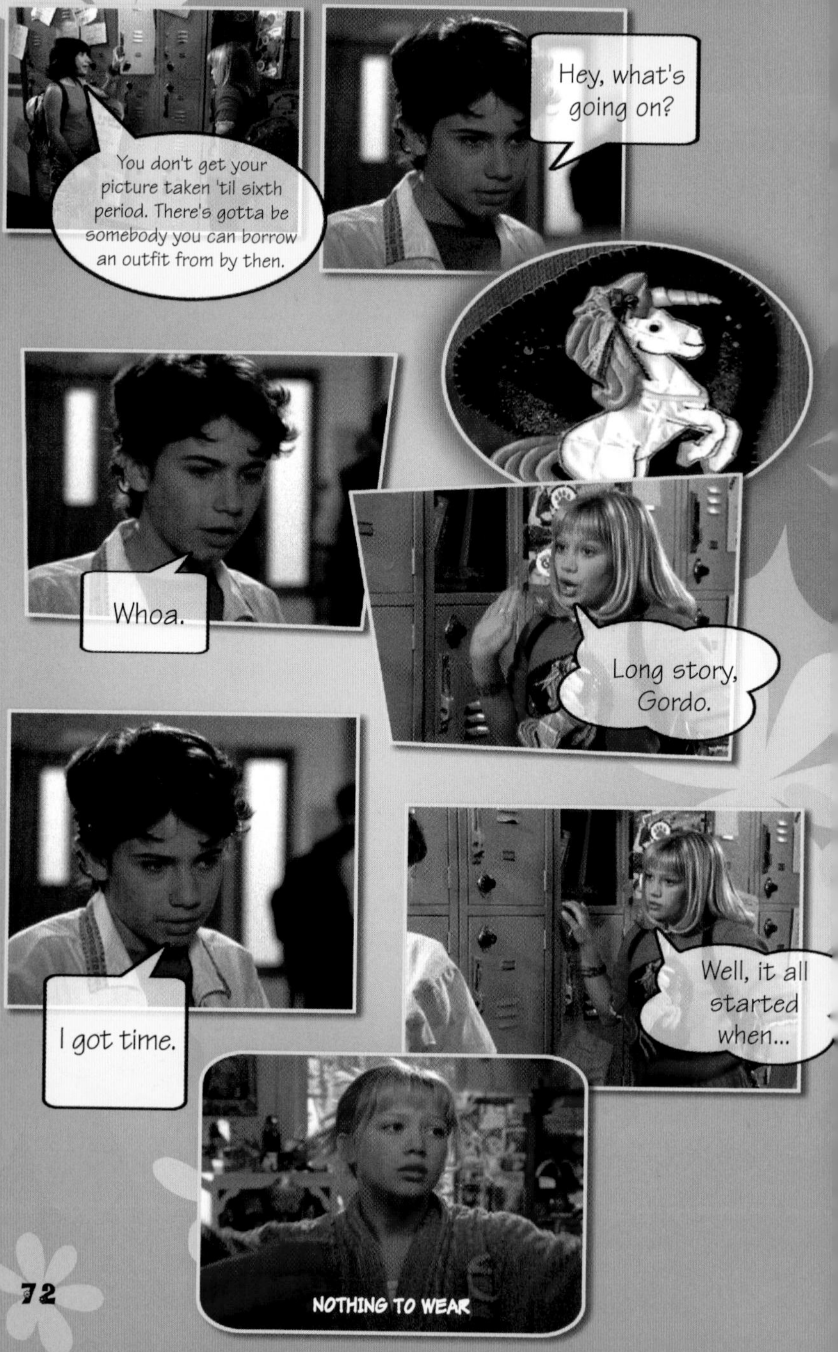
You don't get your picture taken 'til sixth period. There's gotta be somebody you can borrow an outfit from by then.
Hey, what's going on?
Whoa.
Long story, Gordo.
I got time.
Well, it all started when...
NOTHING TO WEAR

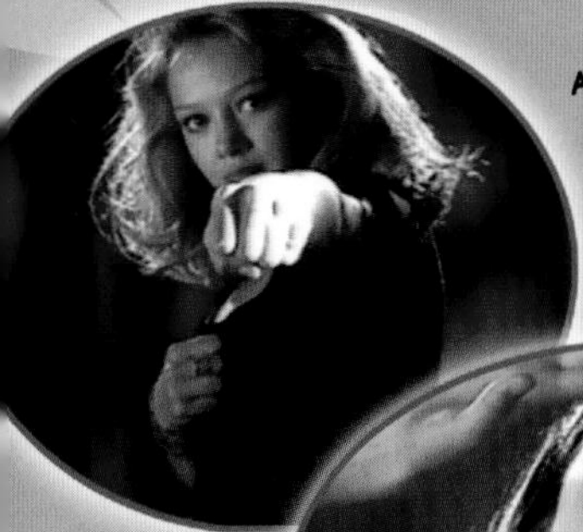

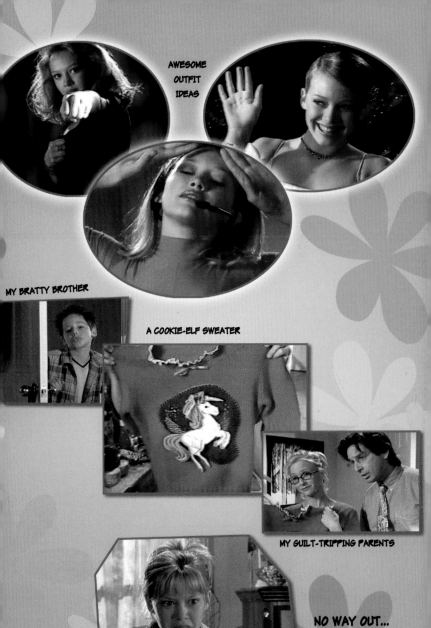

AWESOME OUTFIT IDEAS

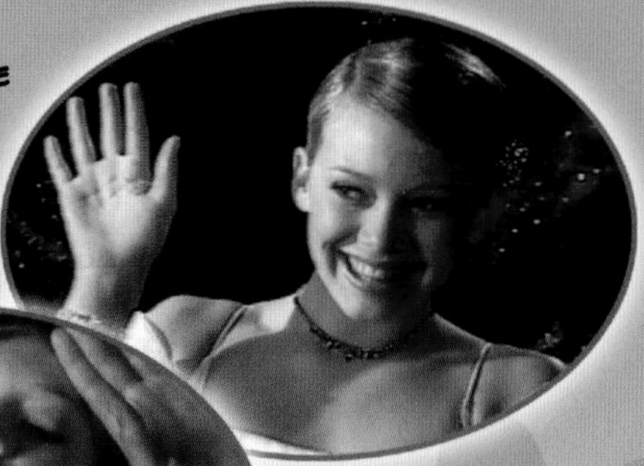

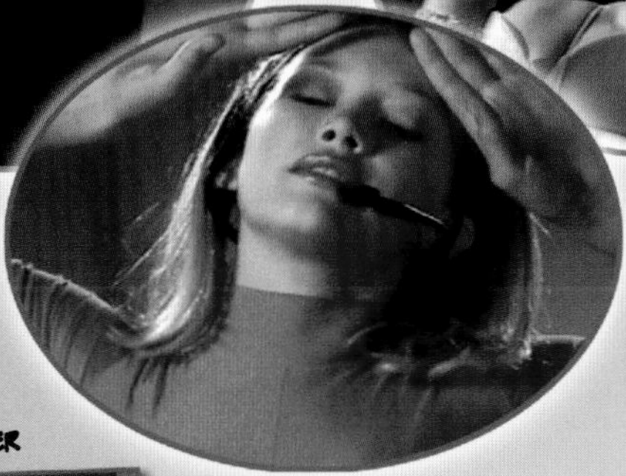

MY BRATTY BROTHER

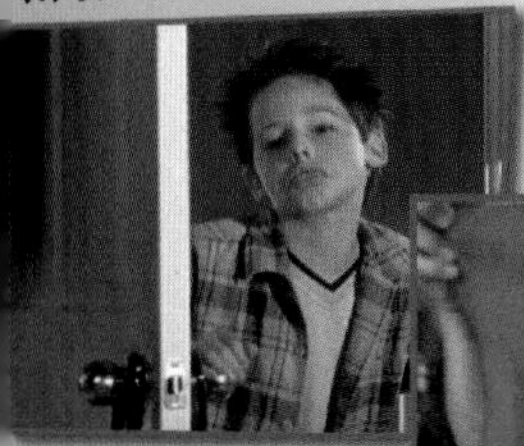

A COOKIE-ELF SWEATER

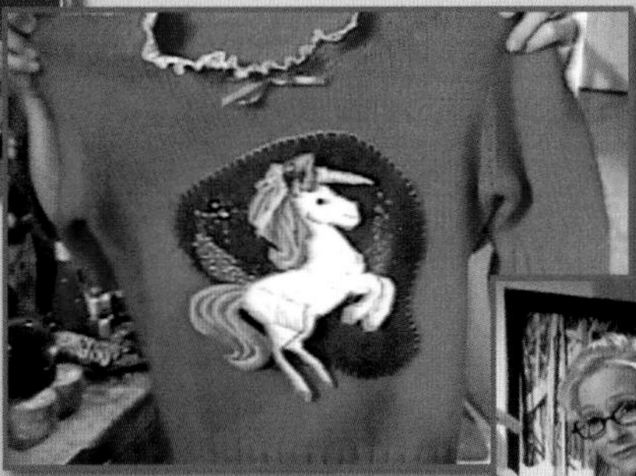

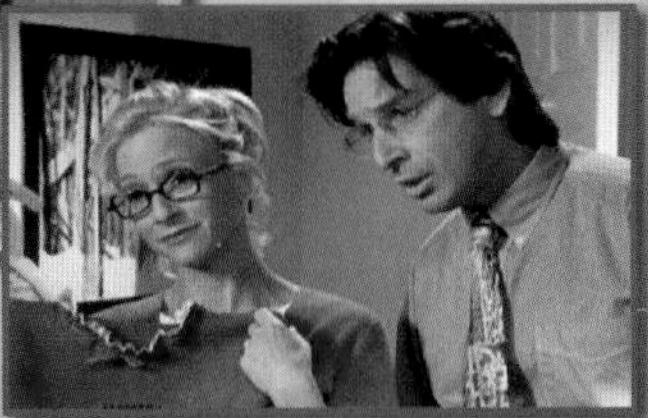

MY GUILT-TRIPPING PARENTS

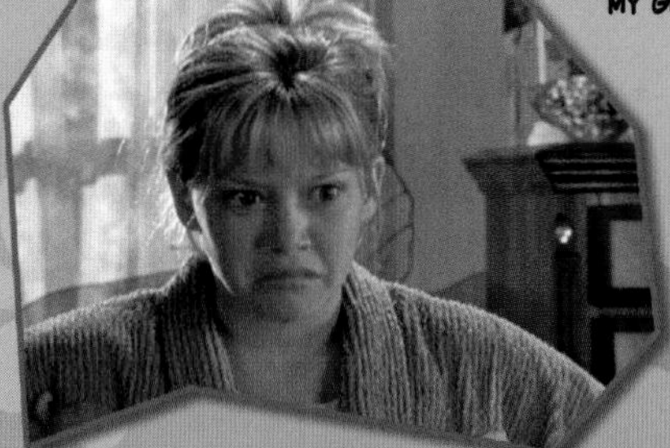

NO WAY OUT...

...AND LAST BUT NOT LEAST, BUS STOP TRAUMA...

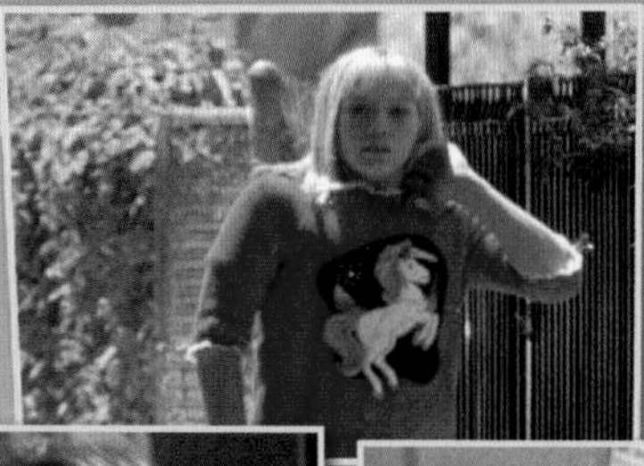

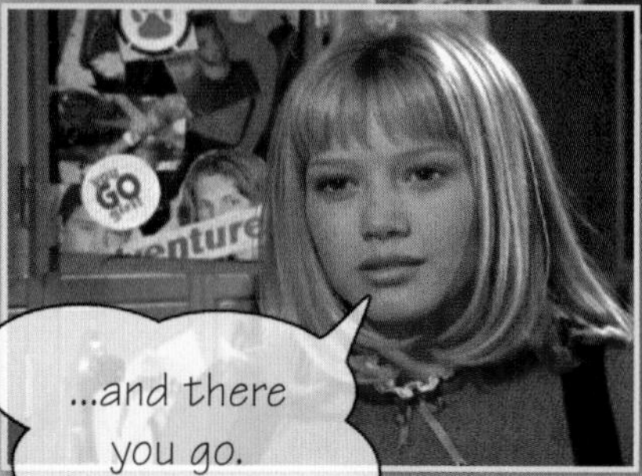
...and there you go.

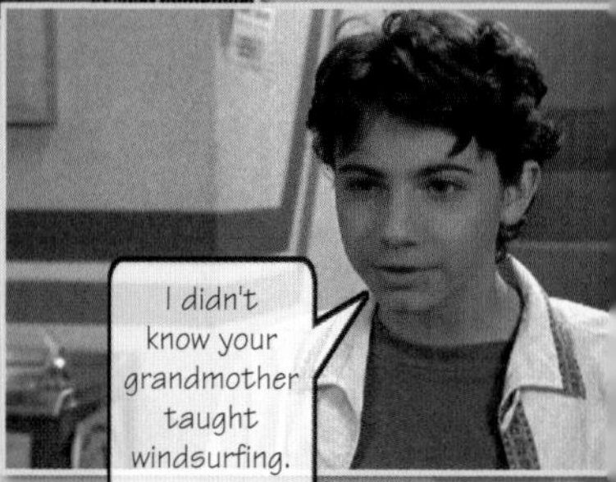
I didn't know your grandmother taught windsurfing.

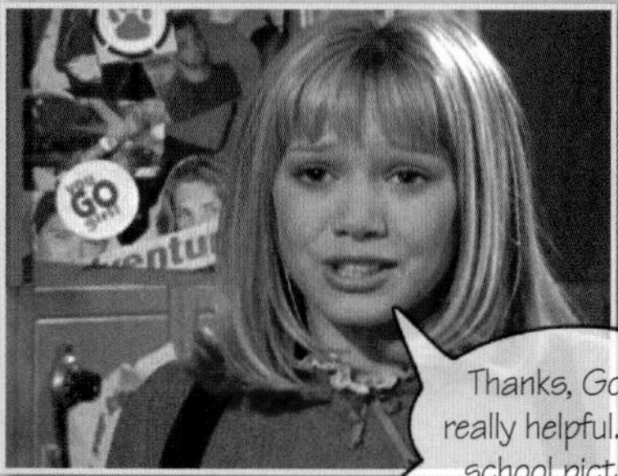
Thanks, Gordo, that's really helpful. Y'know, every school picture I've ever taken has been colossally lame.

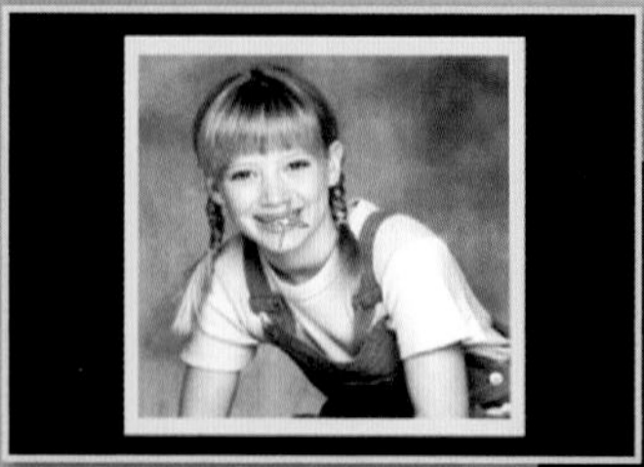

SIXTH GRADE — BRACES.

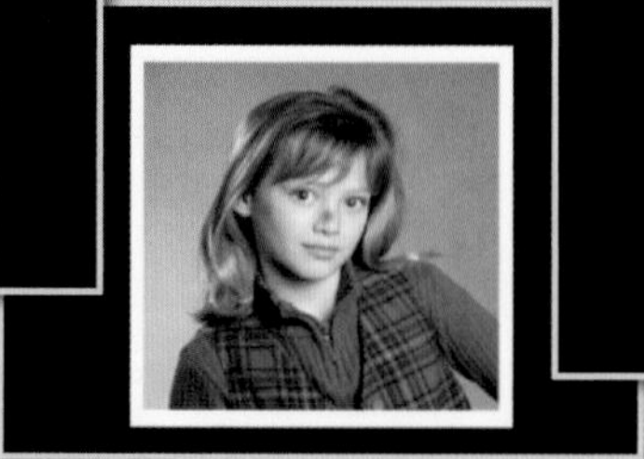

FIFTH GRADE — BEE STING ON MY NOSE.

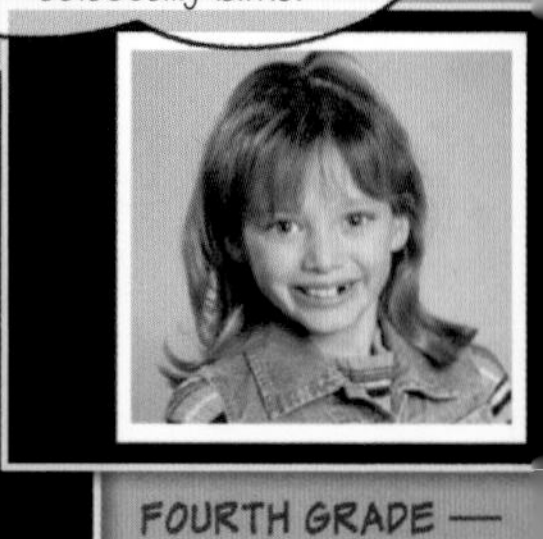

FOURTH GRADE — MISSING TOOTH.

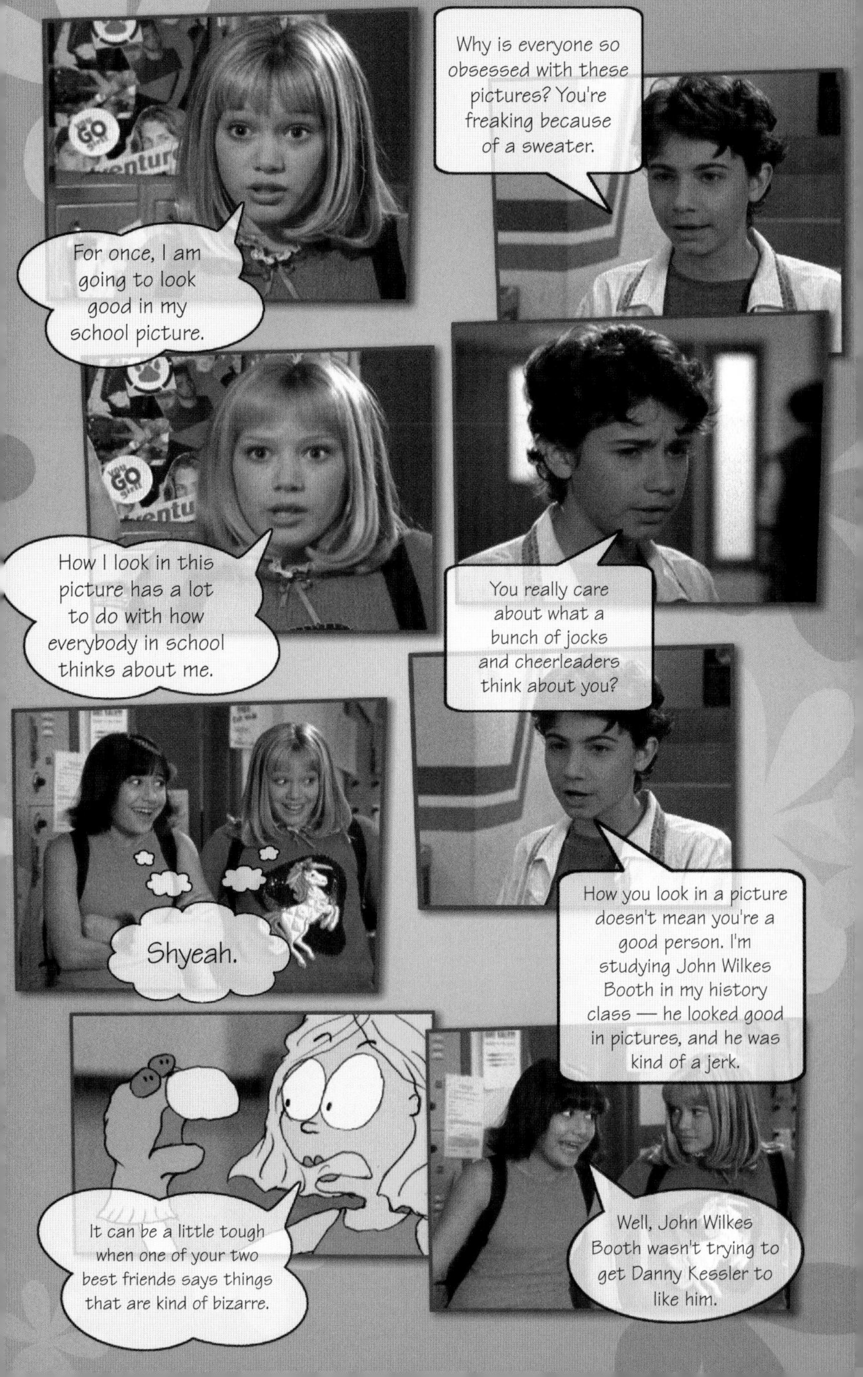
For once, I am going to look good in my school picture.
Why is everyone so obsessed with these pictures? You're freaking because of a sweater.
How I look in this picture has a lot to do with how everybody in school thinks about me.
You really care about what a bunch of jocks and cheerleaders think about you?
Shyeah.
How you look in a picture doesn't mean you're a good person. I'm studying John Wilkes Booth in my history class — he looked good in pictures, and he was kind of a jerk.
It can be a little tough when one of your two best friends says things that are kind of bizarre.
Well, John Wilkes Booth wasn't trying to get Danny Kessler to like him.

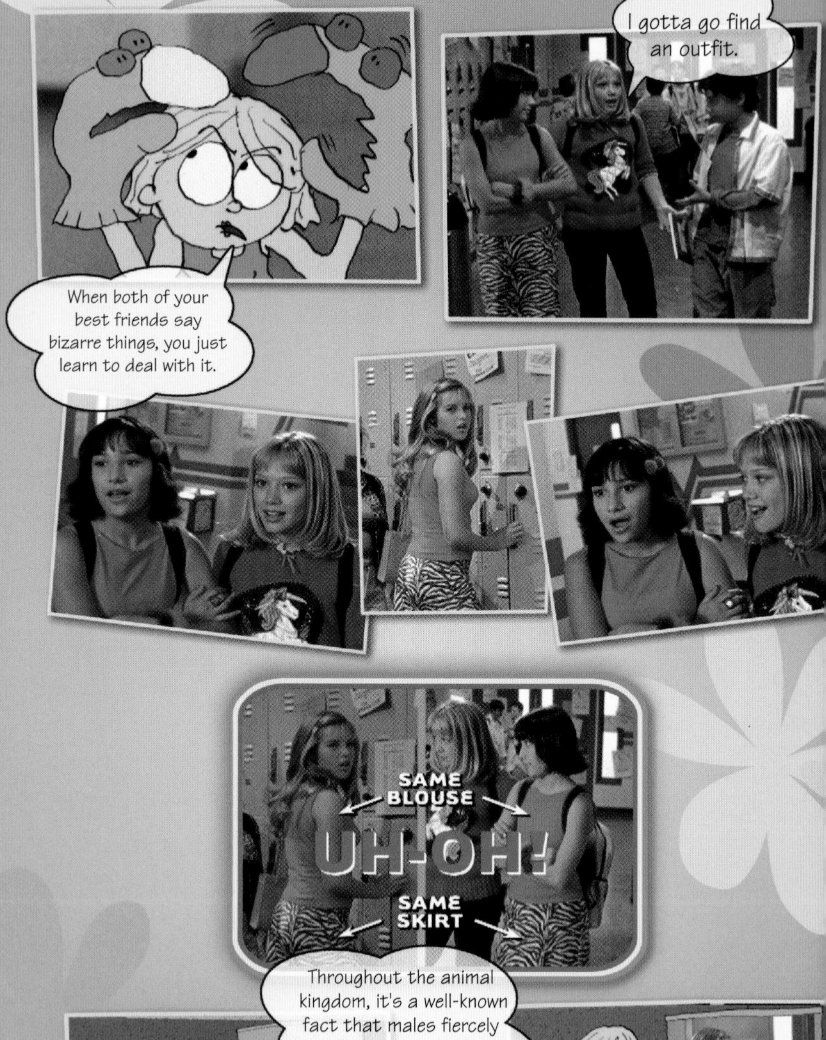
When both of your best friends say bizarre things, you just learn to deal with it.
I gotta go find an outfit.
SAME BLOUSE
UH-OH!
SAME SKIRT
Throughout the animal kingdom, it's a well-known fact that males fiercely compete to establish themselves within the herd.
But in middle school, girls get in on the action, too.

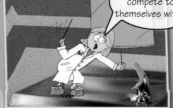

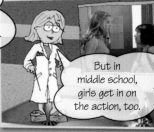

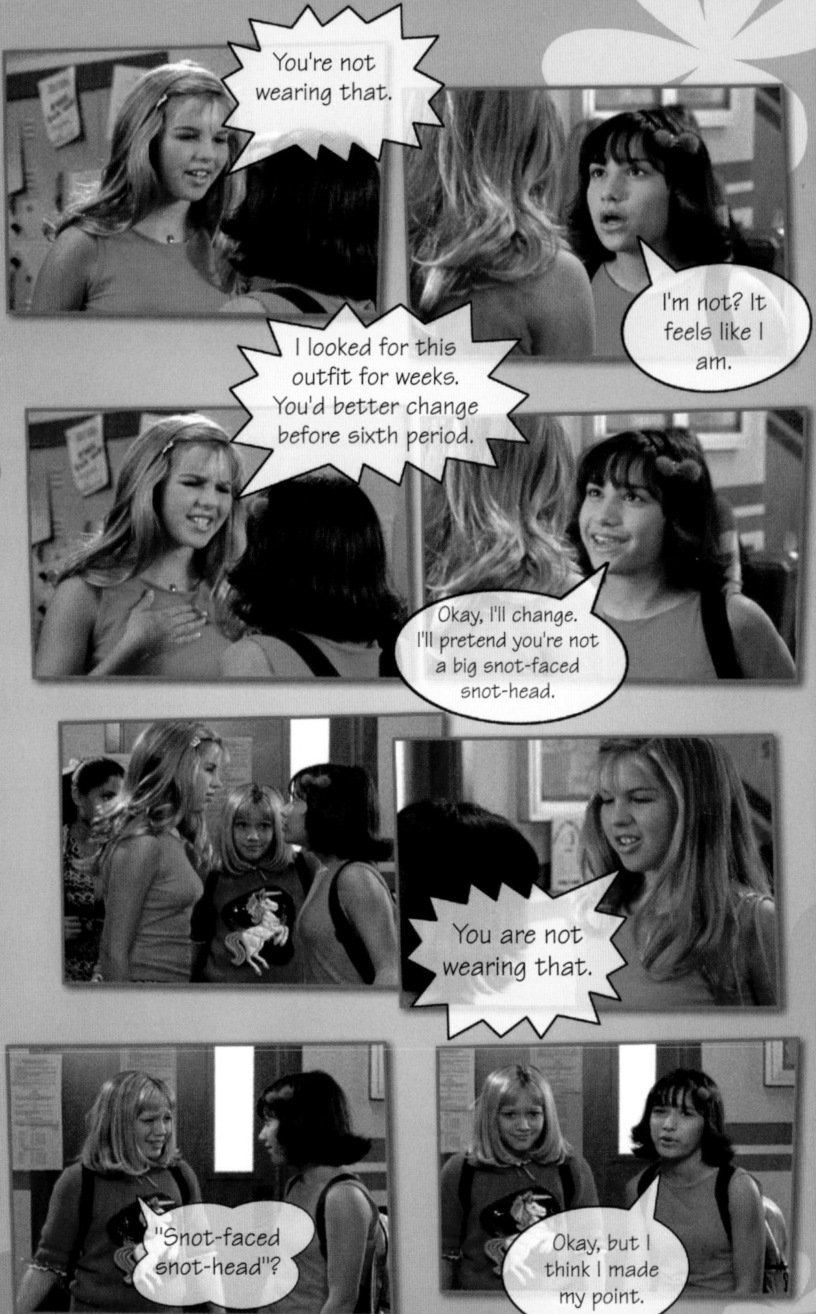
You're not wearing that.
I'm not? It feels like I am.
I looked for this outfit for weeks. You'd better change before sixth period.
Okay, I'll change. I'll pretend you're not a big snot-faced snot-head.
You are not wearing that.
"Snot-faced snot-head"?
Okay, but I think I made my point.

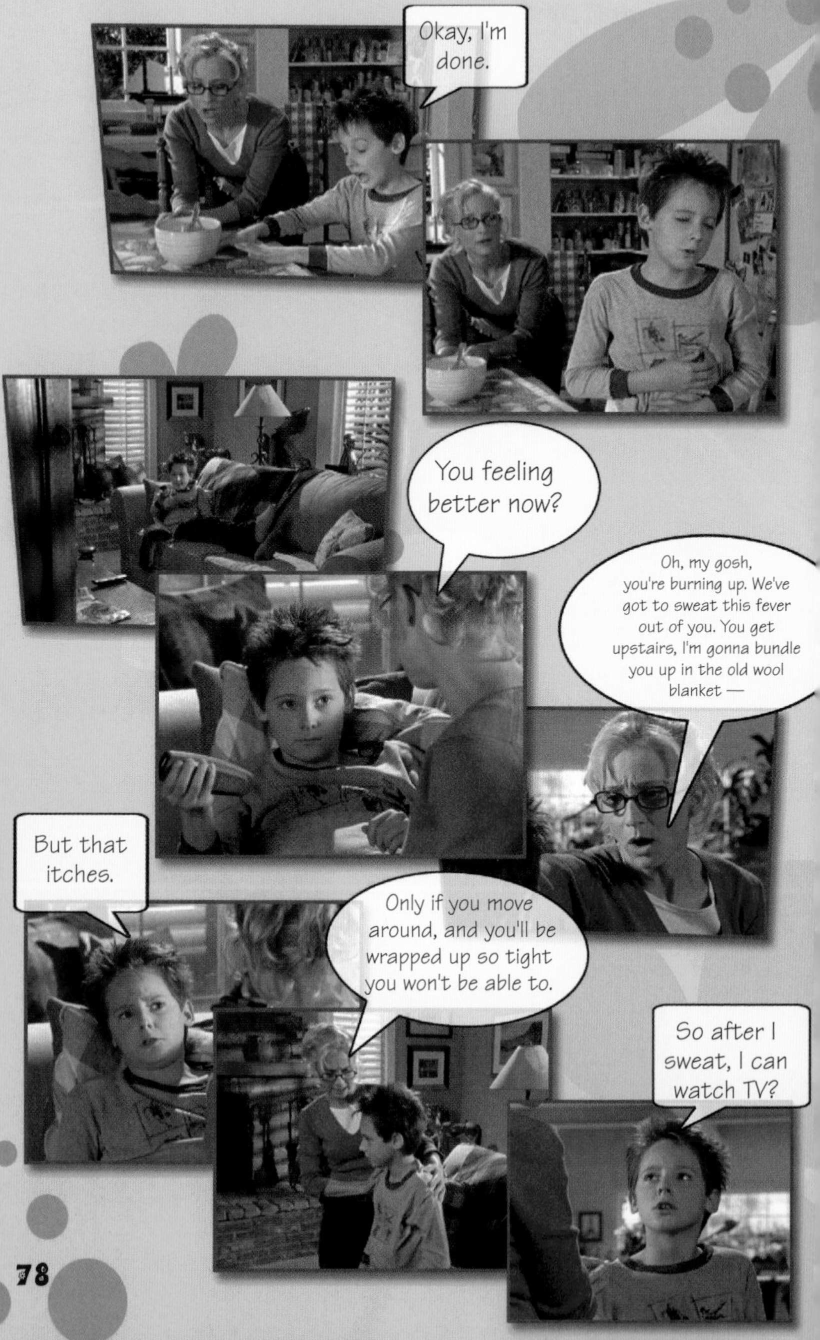
Okay, I'm done.
You feeling better now?
Oh, my gosh, you're burning up. We've got to sweat this fever out of you. You get upstairs, I'm gonna bundle you up in the old wool blanket —
But that itches.
Only if you move around, and you'll be wrapped up so tight you won't be able to.
So after I sweat, I can watch TV?

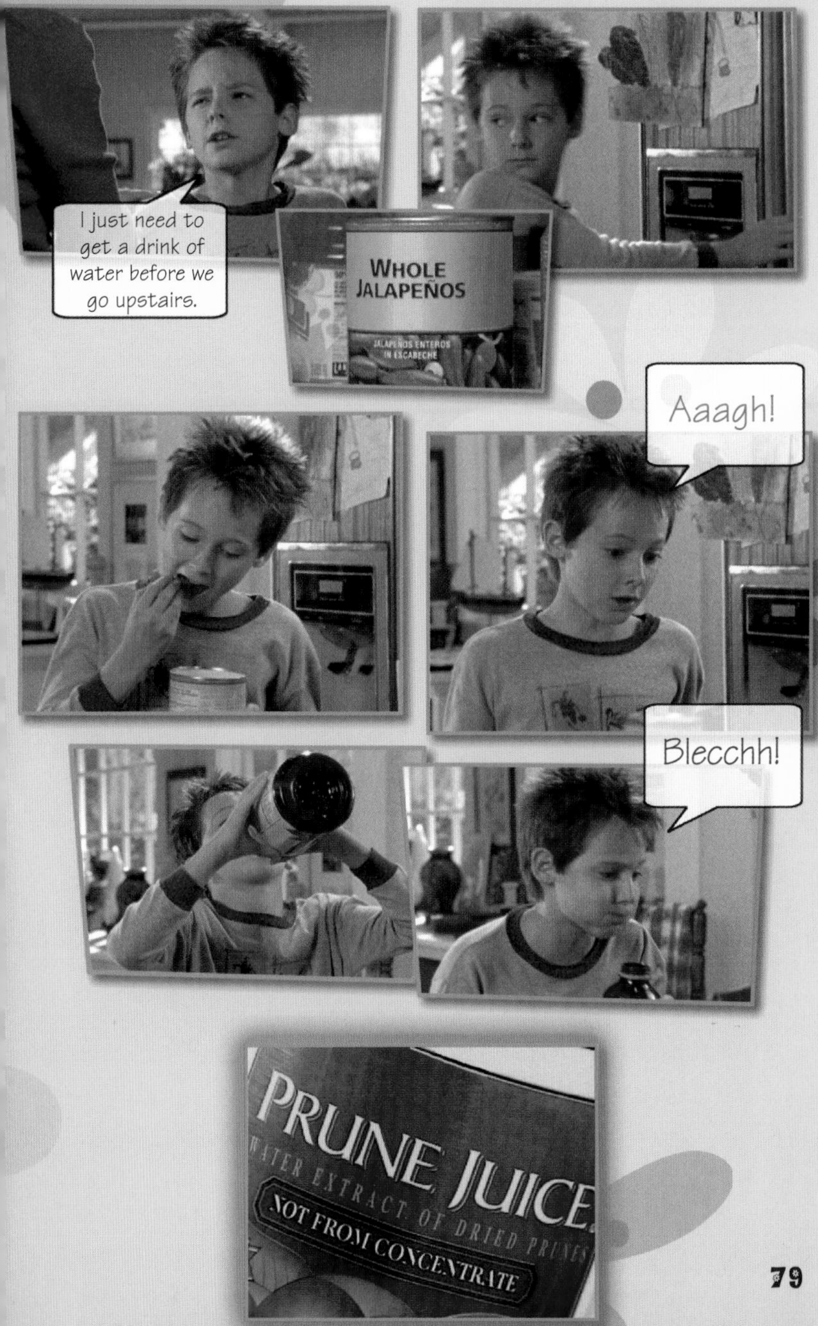
I just need to get a drink of water before we go upstairs.
WHOLE JALAPEÑOS
JALAPEÑOS ENTEROS IN ESCABECHE
Aaagh!
Blecchh!
PRUNE JUICE
WATER EXTRACT OF DRIED PRUNES
NOT FROM CONCENTRATE

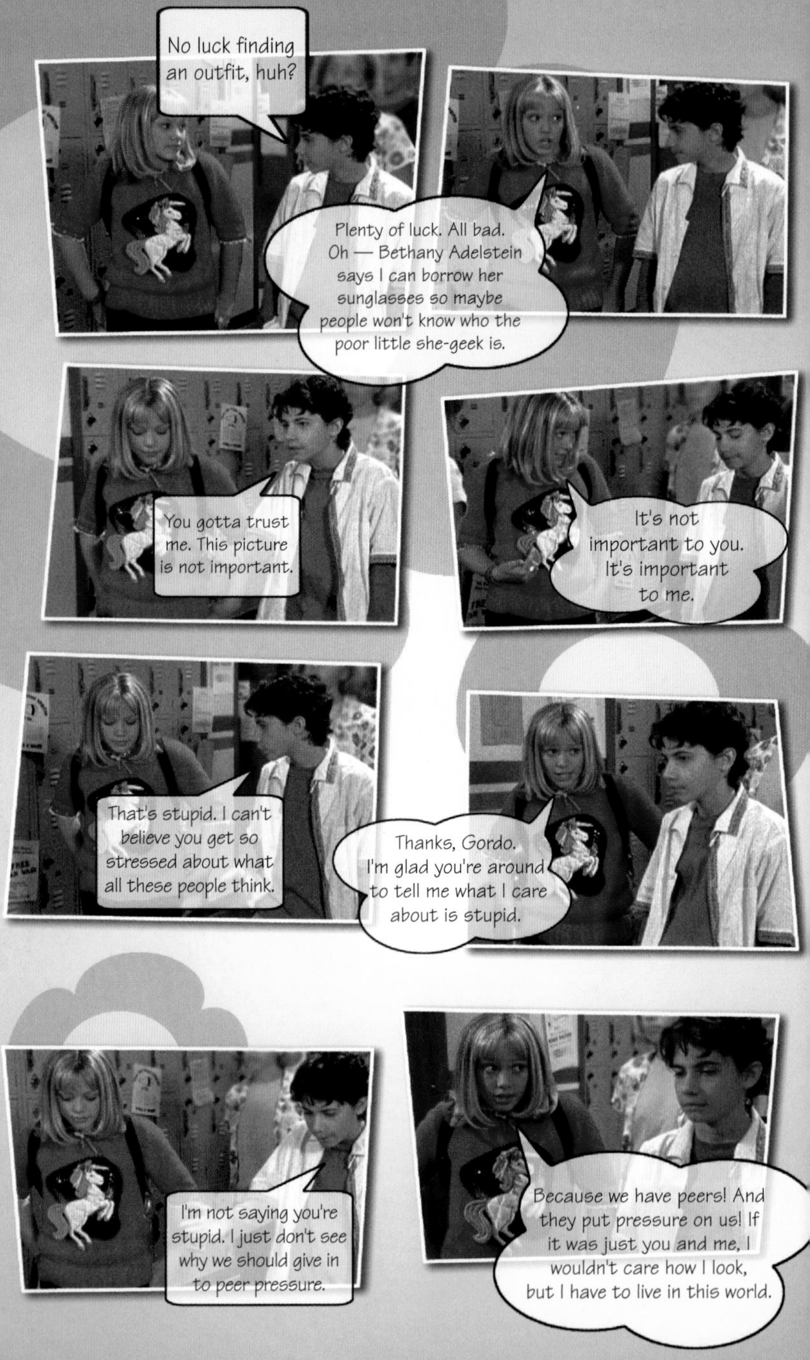
No luck finding an outfit, huh?
Plenty of luck. All bad. Oh — Bethany Adelstein says I can borrow her sunglasses so maybe people won't know who the poor little she-geek is.
You gotta trust me. This picture is not important.
It's not important to you. It's important to me.
That's stupid. I can't believe you get so stressed about what all these people think.
Thanks, Gordo. I'm glad you're around to tell me what I care about is stupid.
I'm not saying you're stupid. I just don't see why we should give in to peer pressure.
Because we have peers! And they put pressure on us! If it was just you and me, I wouldn't care how I look, but I have to live in this world.

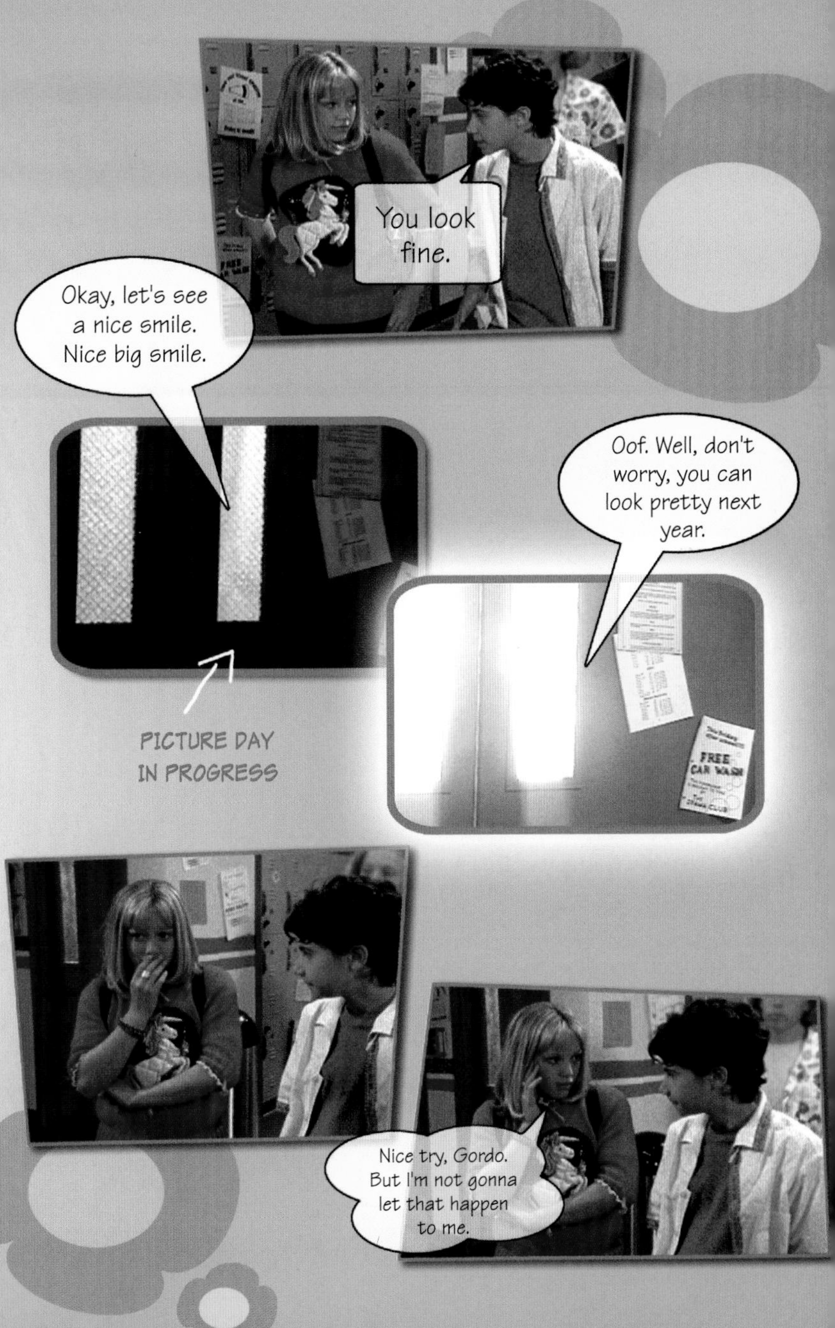

You look fine.
Okay, let's see a nice smile. Nice big smile.
PICTURE DAY IN PROGRESS
Oof. Well, don't worry, you can look pretty next year.
Nice try, Gordo. But I'm not gonna let that happen to me.

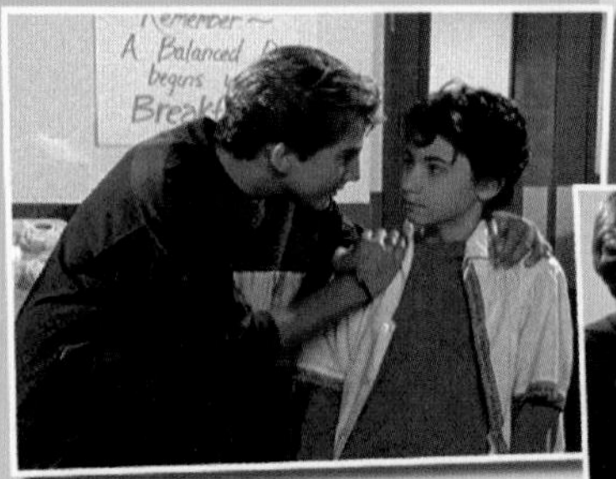

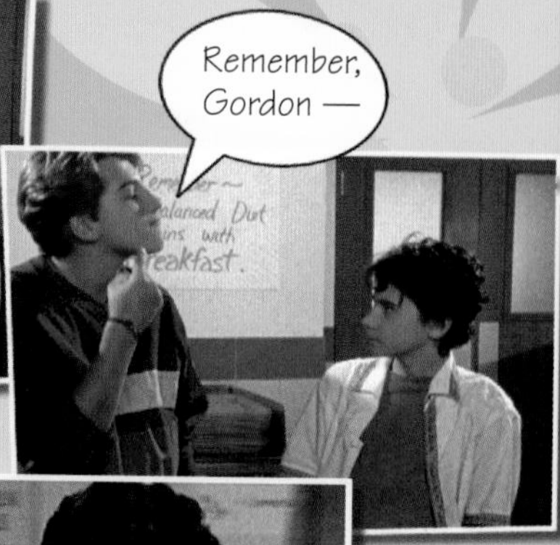
Remember, Gordon —

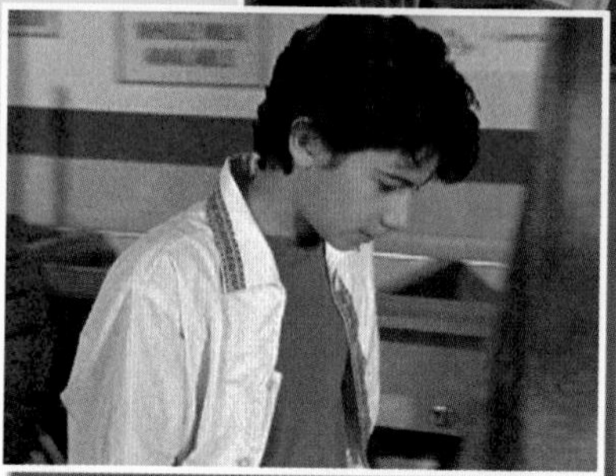

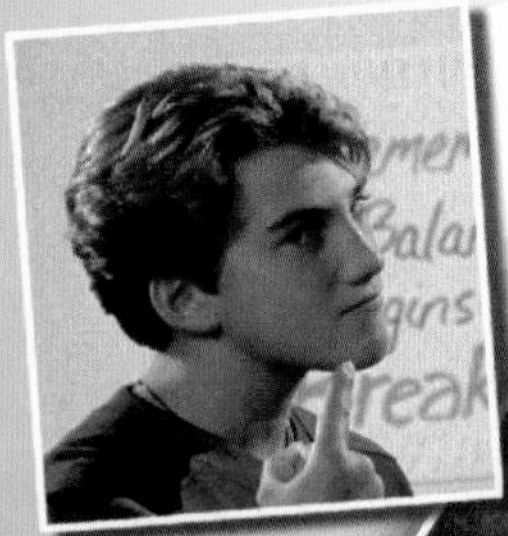

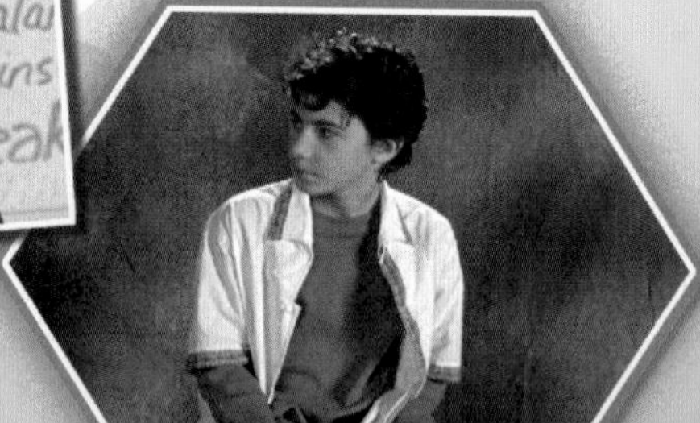

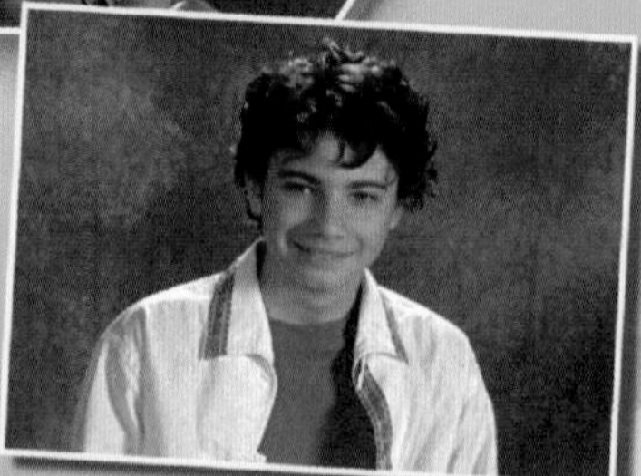

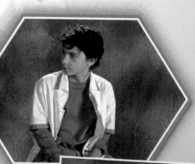

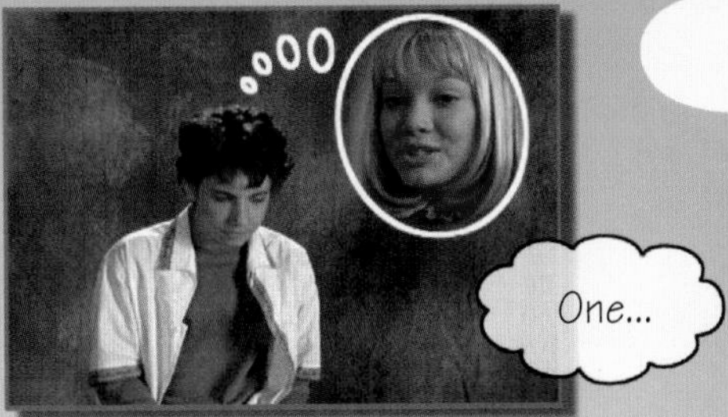
One...

HOW THIS PICTURE COMES OUT HAS A LOT TO DO WITH HOW EVERYBODY IN SCHOOL THINKS ABOUT ME.

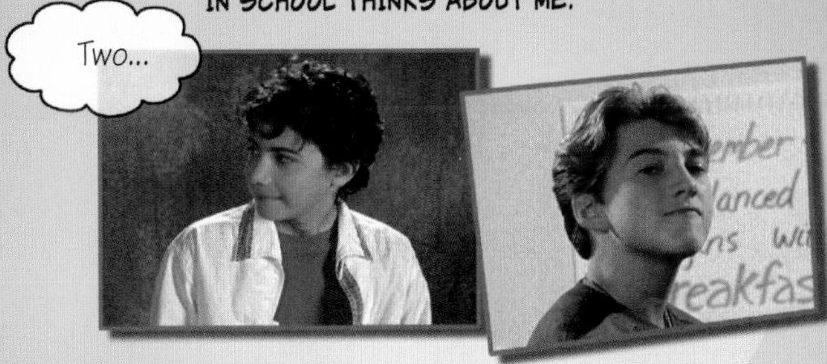
Two...

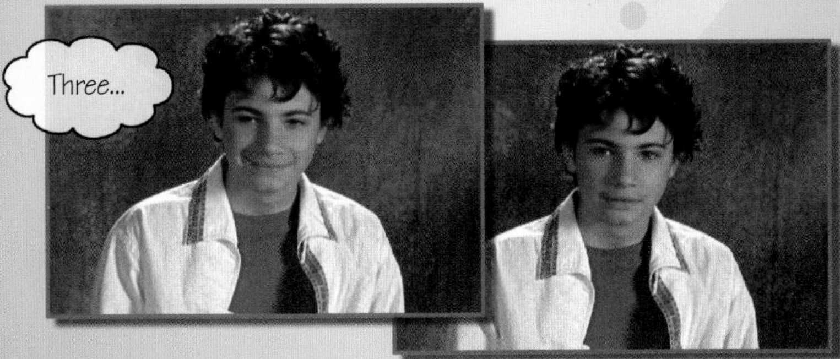
Three...

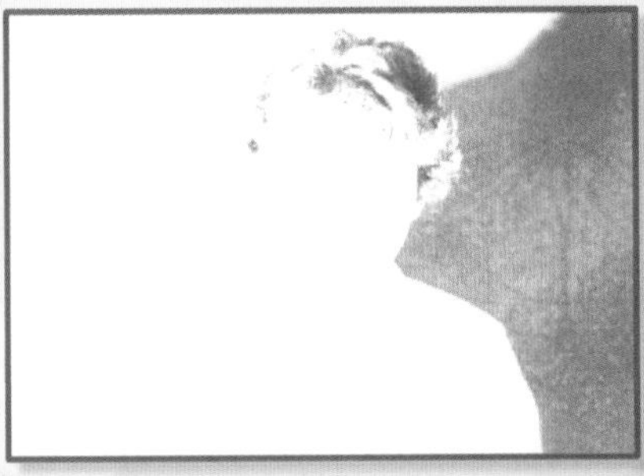

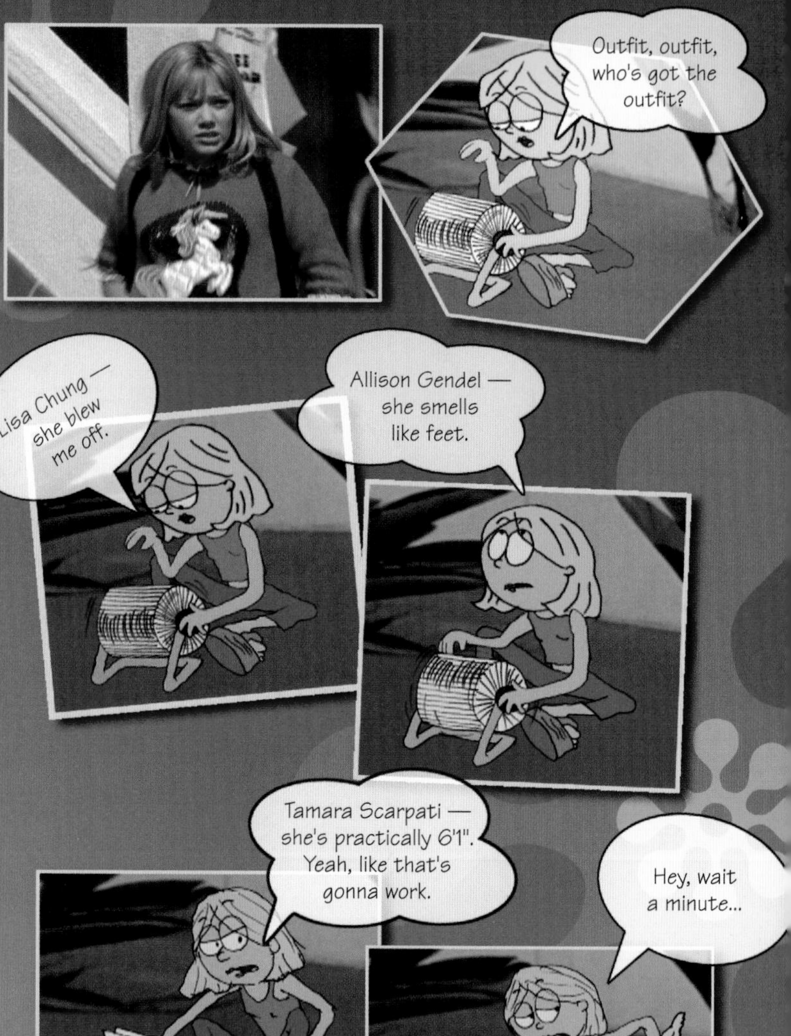
Outfit, outfit, who's got the outfit?
Lisa Chung — she blew me off.
Allison Gendel — she smells like feet.
Tamara Scarpati — she's practically 6'1". Yeah, like that's gonna work.
Hey, wait a minute...

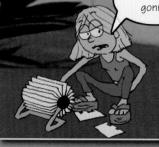

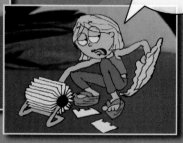

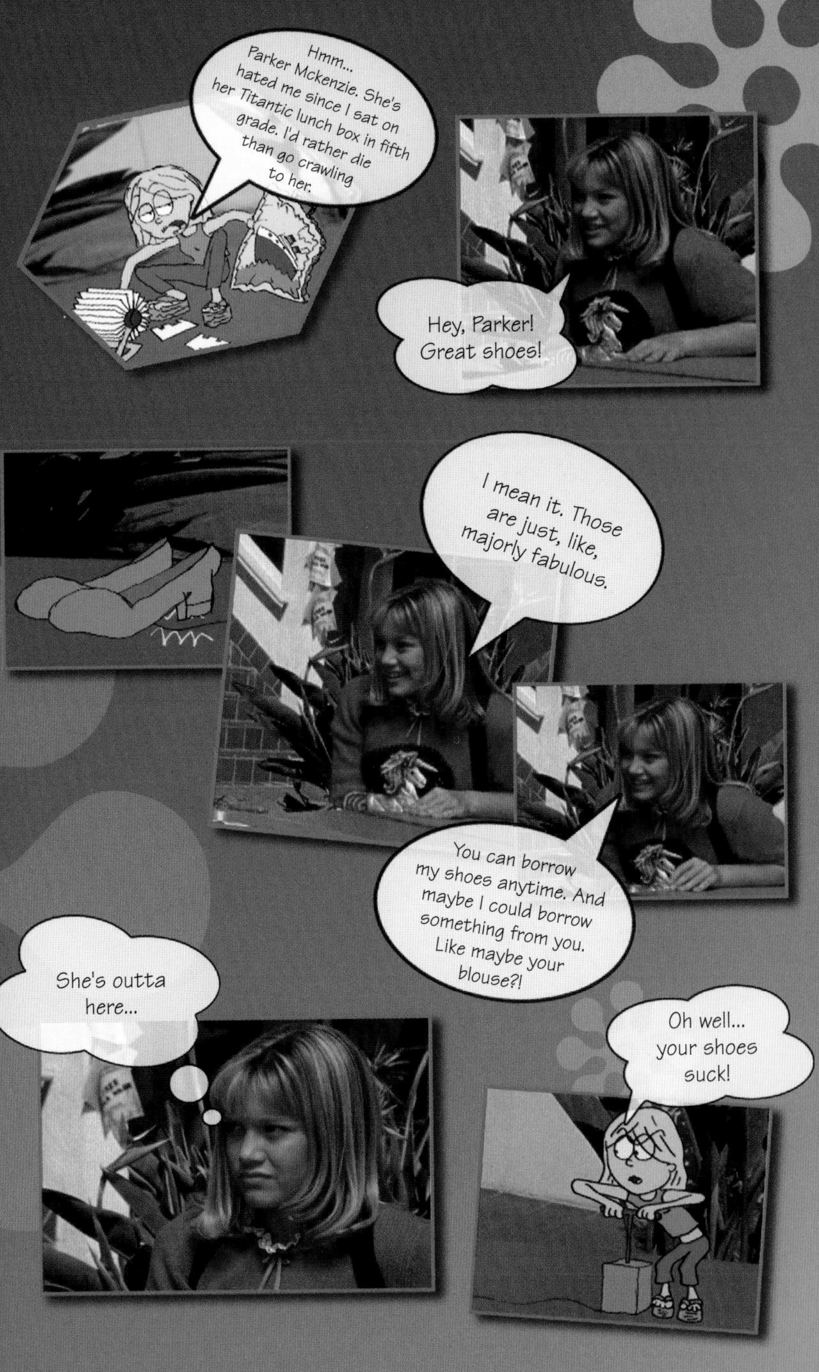
Hmm... Parker Mckenzie. She's hated me since I sat on her Titanic lunch box in fifth grade. I'd rather die than go crawling to her.
Hey, Parker! Great shoes!
I mean it. Those are just, like, majorly fabulous.
You can borrow my shoes anytime. And maybe I could borrow something from you. Like maybe your blouse?!
She's outta here...
Oh well... your shoes suck!

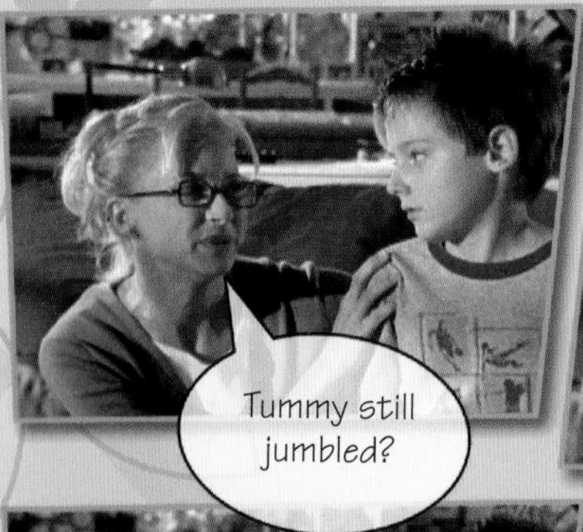
Tummy still jumbled?

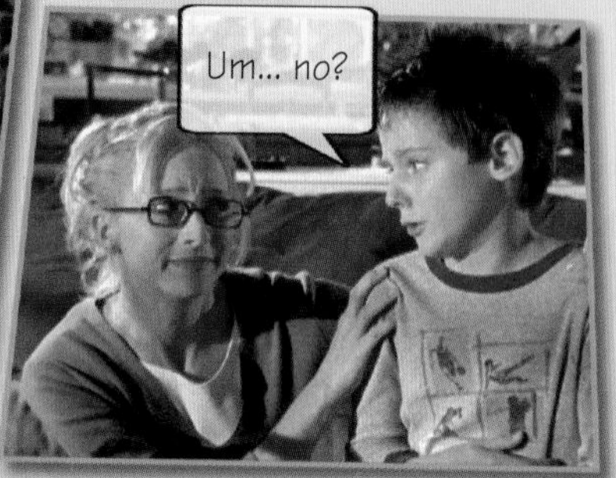
Um... no?

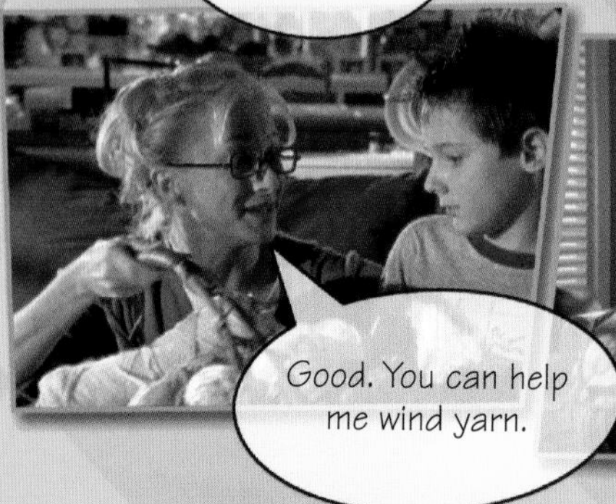
Good. You can help me wind yarn.

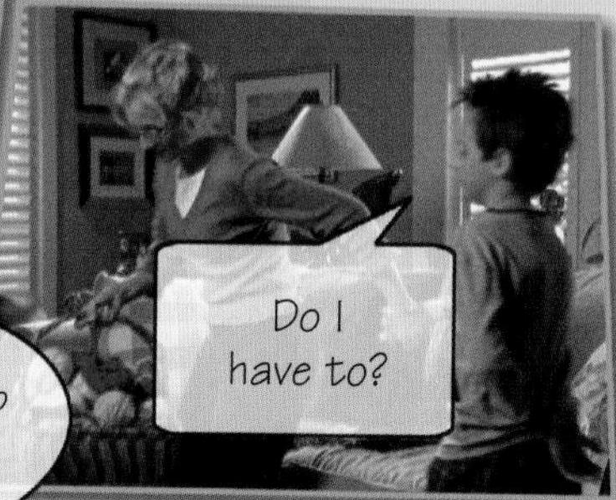
Do I have to?

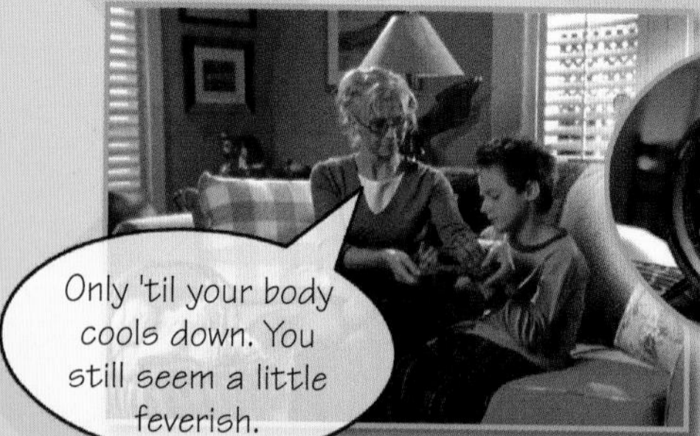
Only 'til your body cools down. You still seem a little feverish.

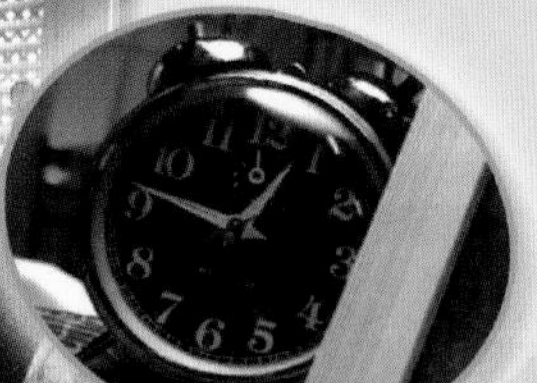

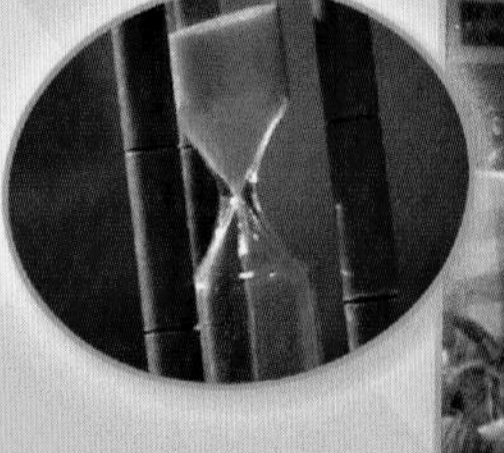

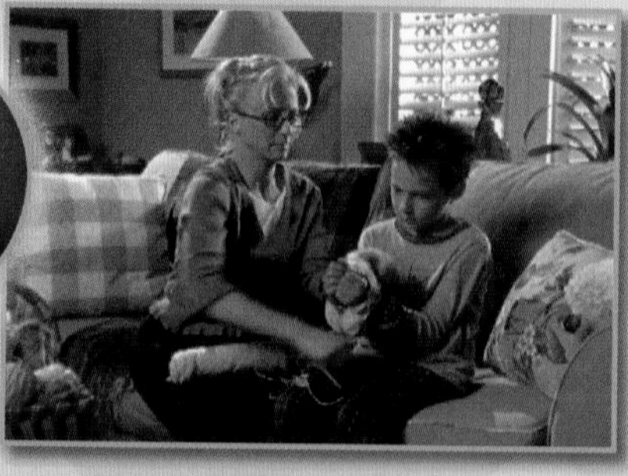

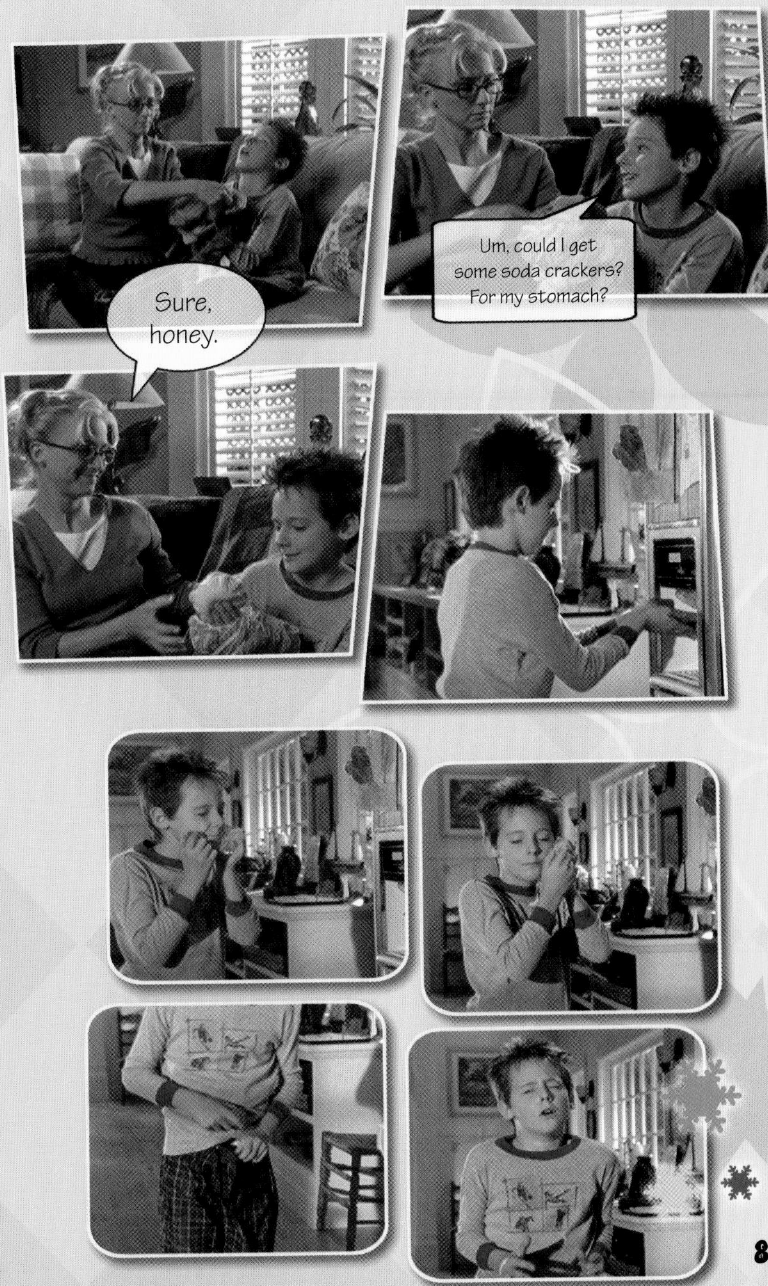
Um, could I get some soda crackers? For my stomach?
Sure, honey.

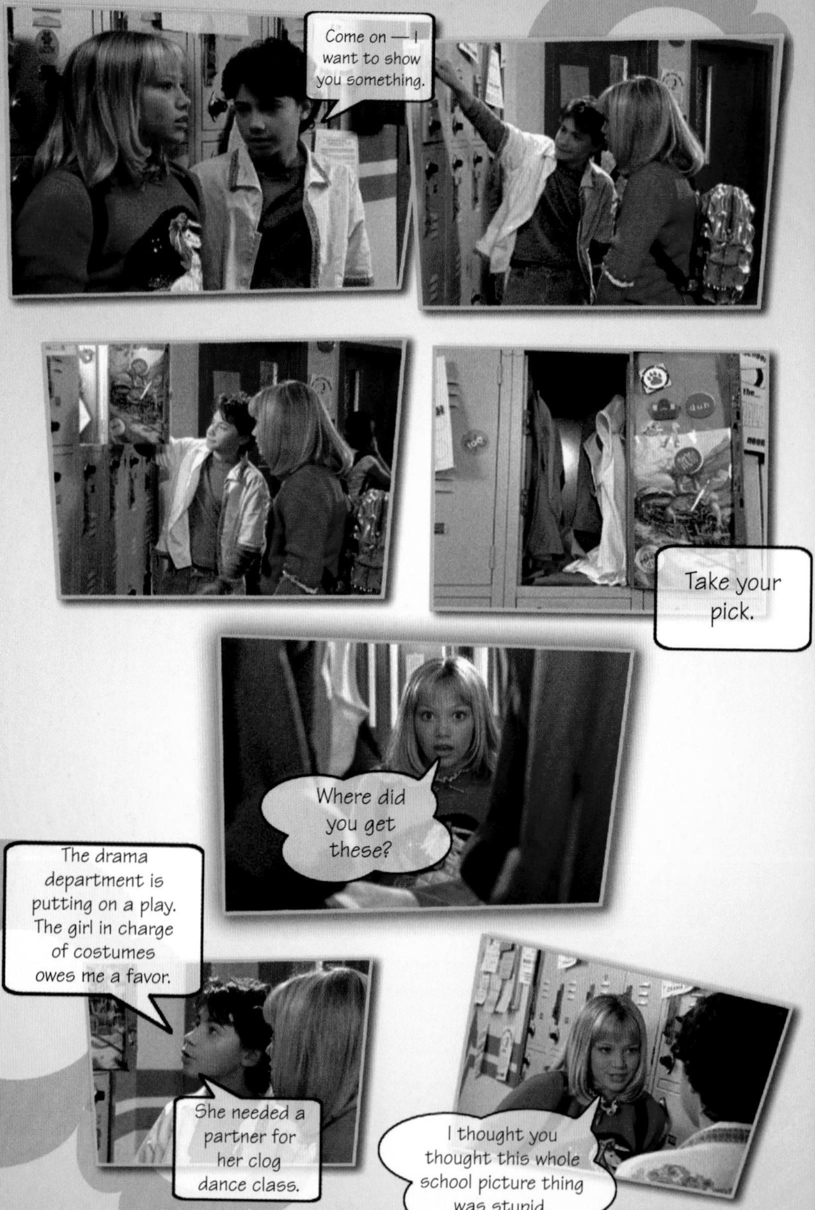
Come on — I want to show you something.
Take your pick.
Where did you get these?
The drama department is putting on a play. The girl in charge of costumes owes me a favor.
She needed a partner for her clog dance class.
I thought you thought this whole school picture thing was stupid.

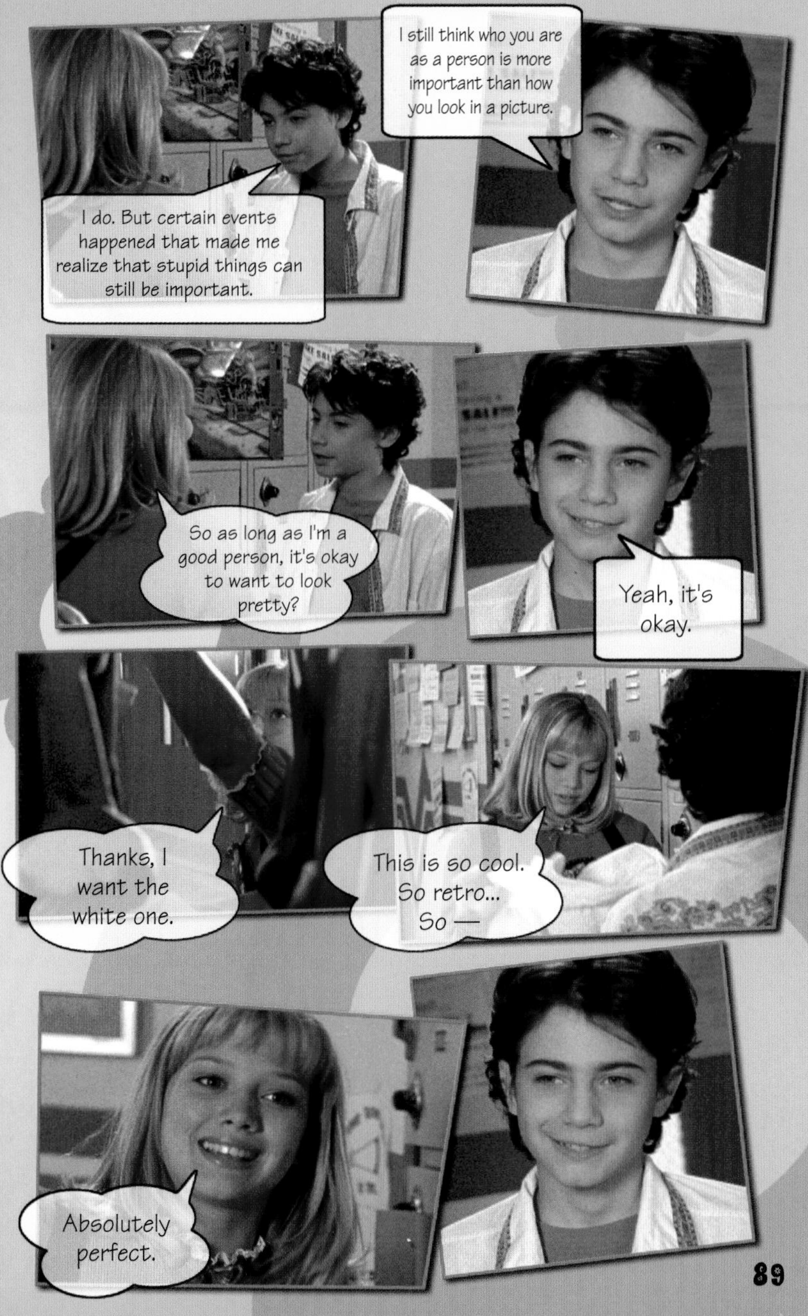
I do. But certain events happened that made me realize that stupid things can still be important.
I still think who you are as a person is more important than how you look in a picture.
So as long as I'm a good person, it's okay to want to look pretty?
Yeah, it's okay.
Thanks, I want the white one.
This is so cool. So retro... So —
Absolutely perfect.

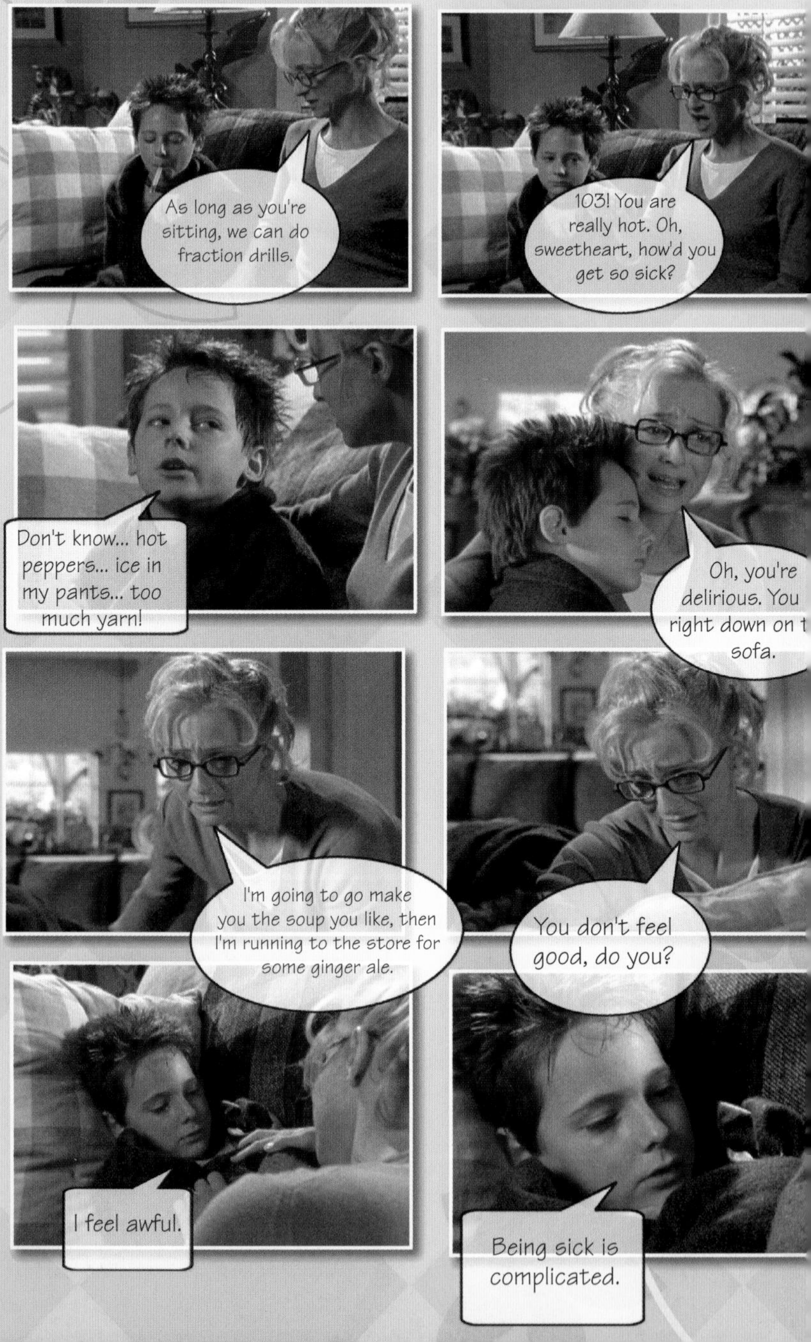
As long as you're sitting, we can do fraction drills.
103! You are really hot. Oh, sweetheart, how'd you get so sick?
Don't know... hot peppers... ice in my pants... too much yarn!
Oh, you're delirious. You right down on t sofa.
I'm going to go make you the soup you like, then I'm running to the store for some ginger ale.
You don't feel good, do you?
I feel awful.
Being sick is complicated.

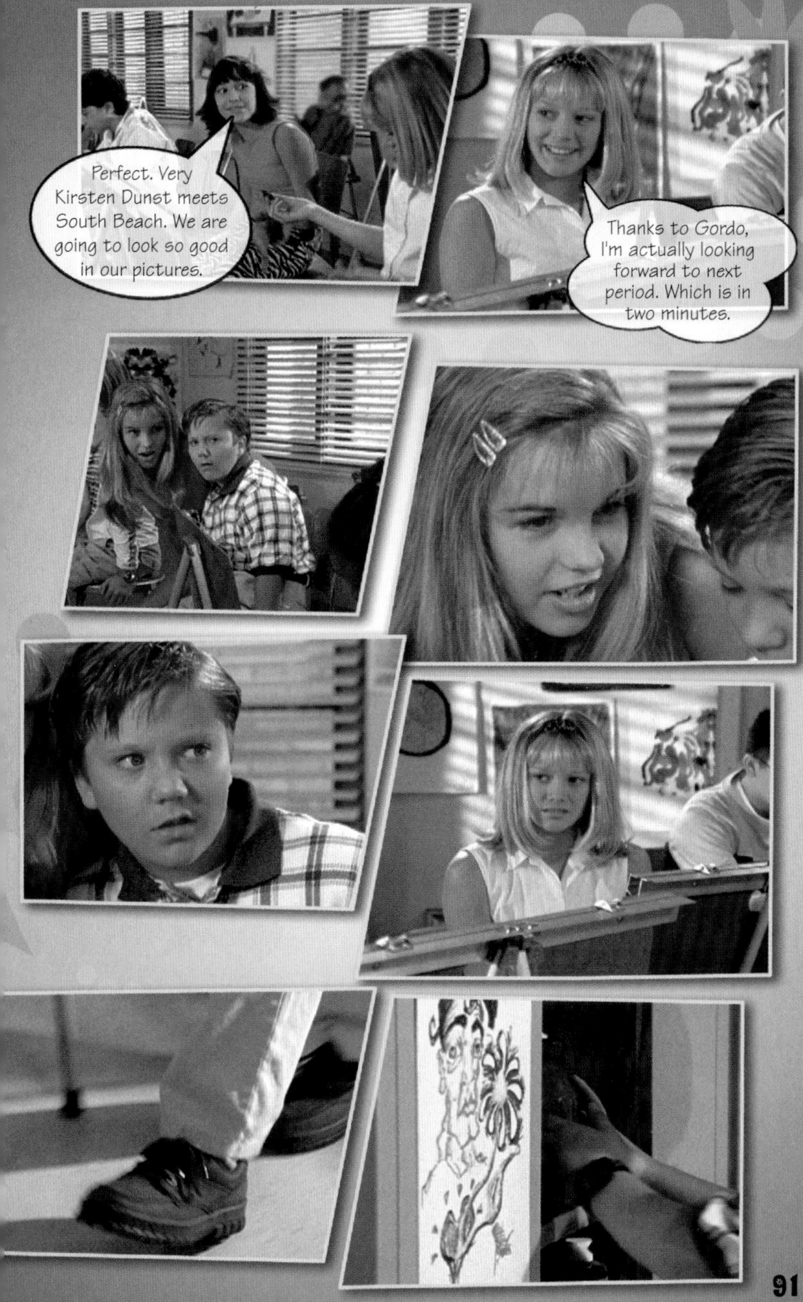
Perfect. Very Kirsten Dunst meets South Beach. We are going to look so good in our pictures.
Thanks to Gordo, I'm actually looking forward to next period. Which is in two minutes.

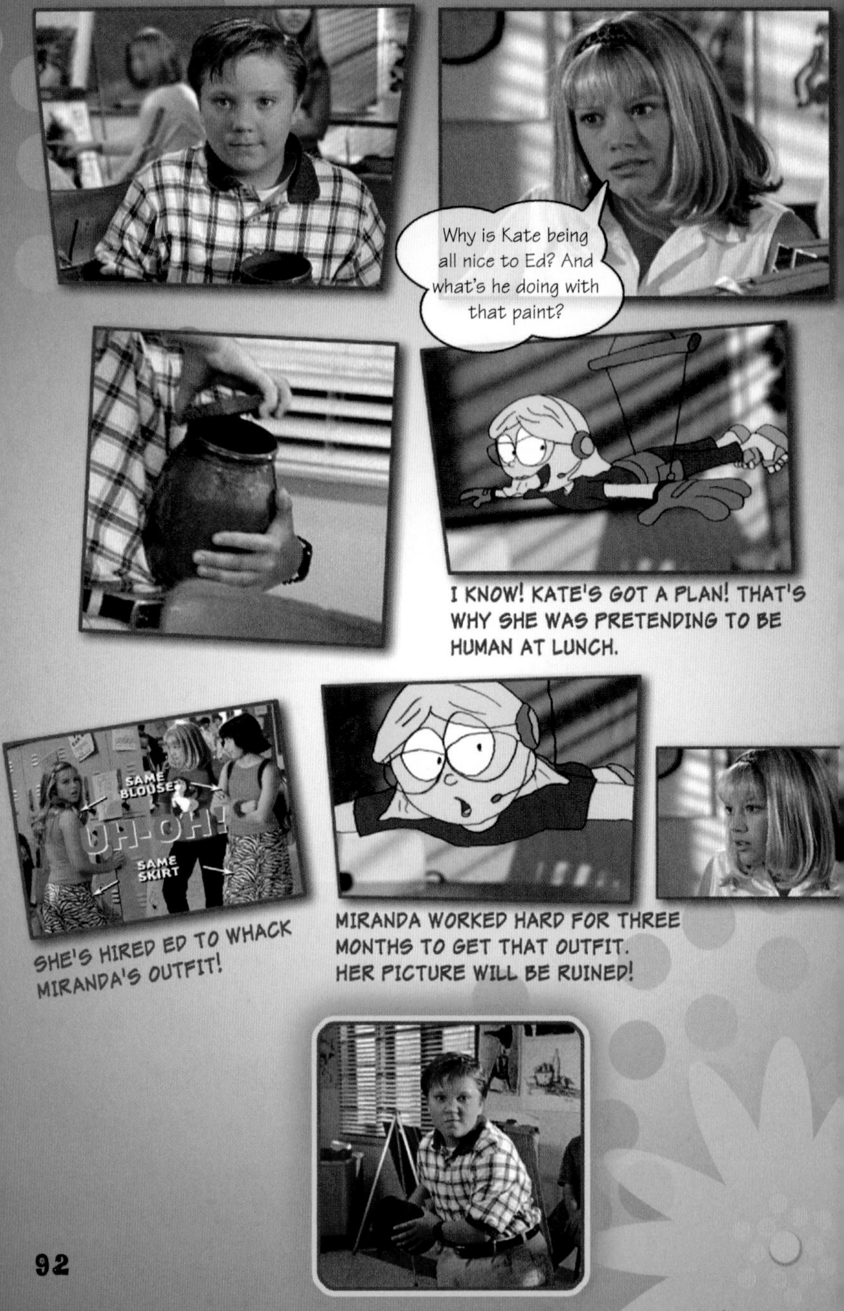
Why is Kate being all nice to Ed? And what's he doing with that paint?
I KNOW! KATE'S GOT A PLAN! THAT'S WHY SHE WAS PRETENDING TO BE HUMAN AT LUNCH.
SAME BLOUSE
UH-OH!
SAME SKIRT
SHE'S HIRED ED TO WHACK MIRANDA'S OUTFIT!
MIRANDA WORKED HARD FOR THREE MONTHS TO GET THAT OUTFIT. HER PICTURE WILL BE RUINED!

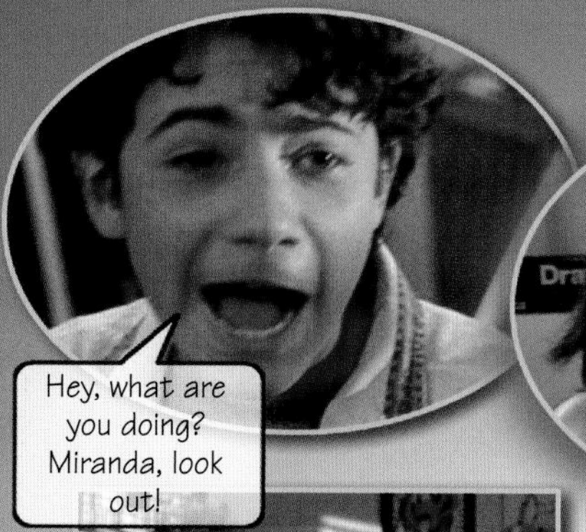
Hey, what are you doing? Miranda, look out!

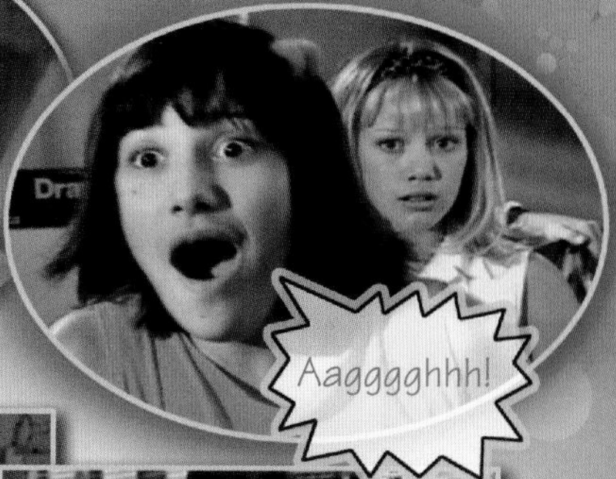
Aagggghhh!

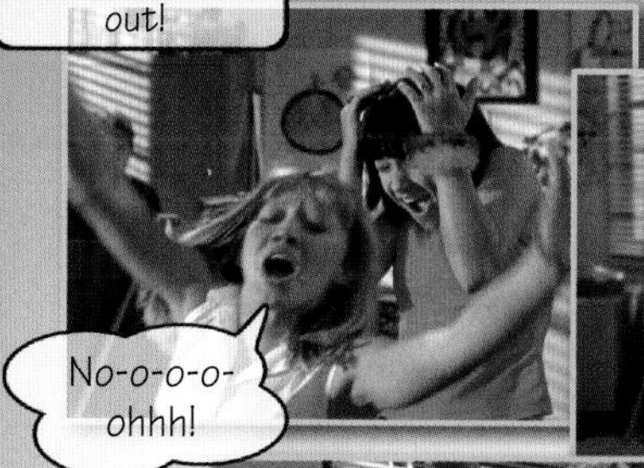
No-o-o-o-ohhh!

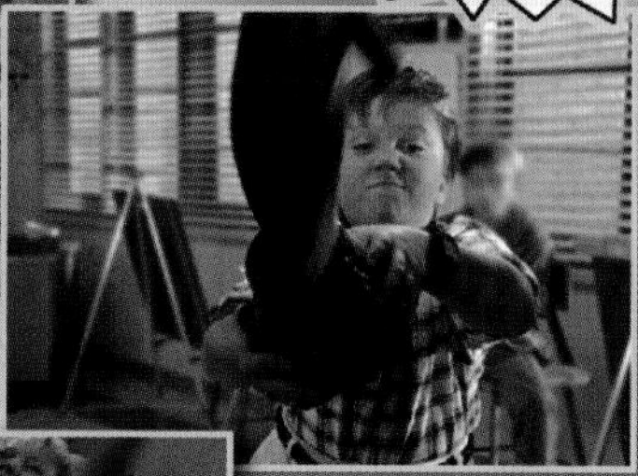

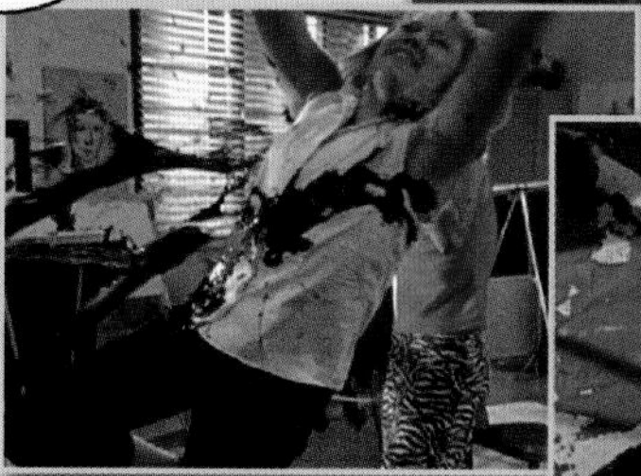

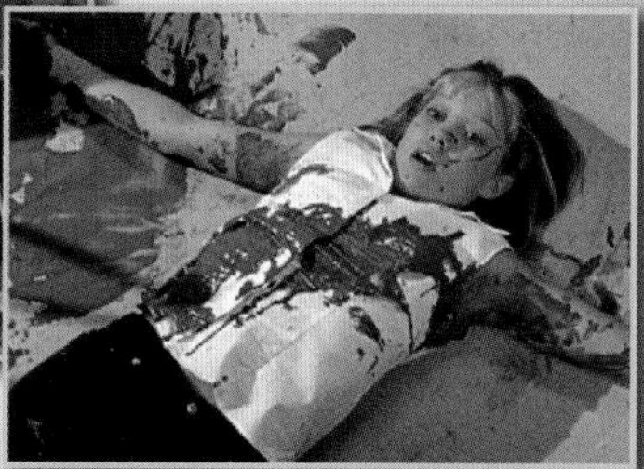

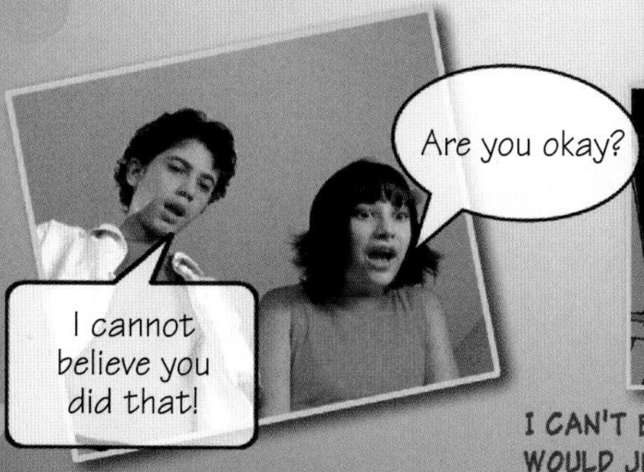
Are you okay?
I cannot believe you did that!

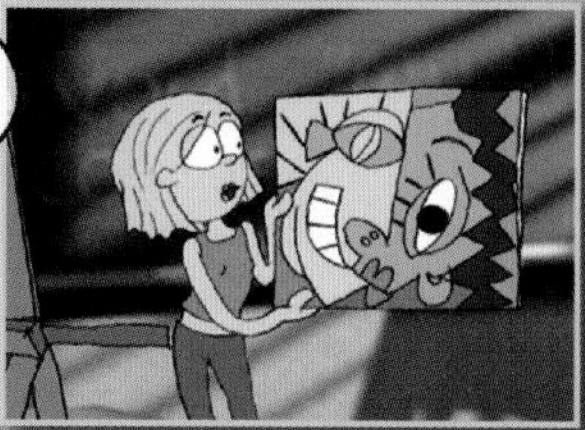

I CAN'T BELIEVE IT, EITHER. BUT MIRANDA WOULD JUMP ON A PAINT GRENADE FOR ME. BESIDES, GREEN'S VERY IN THIS SEASON. AND IT'S NOT LIKE I WAS THE ONLY ONE WHOSE PICTURE CAME OUT WEIRD.

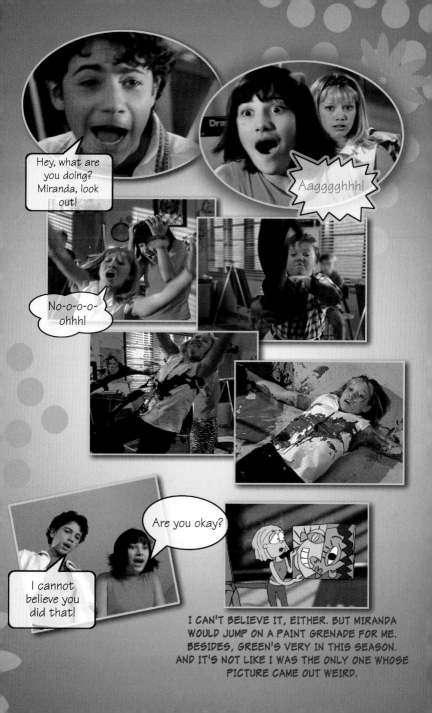

KATE SNEEZED...

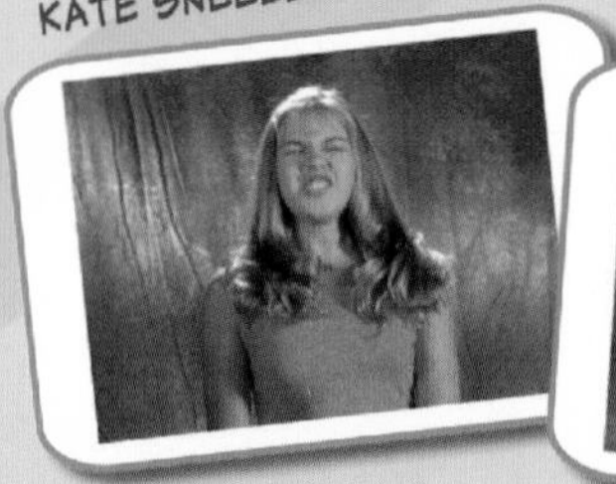

ETHAN SMILED...

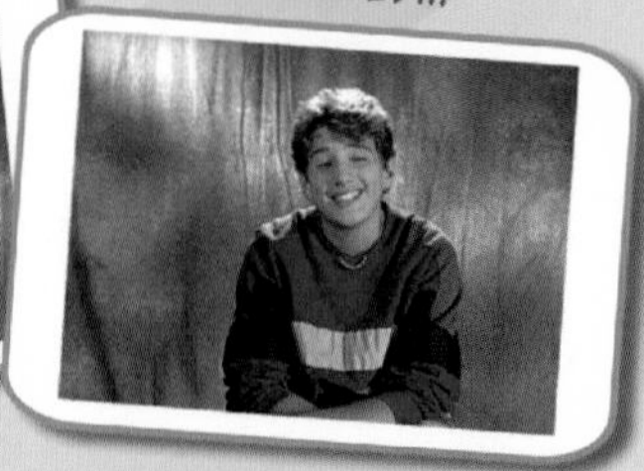

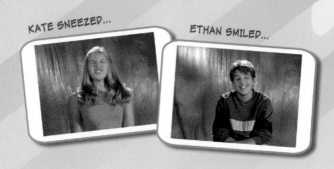

...BUT MIRANDA LOOKED WAY AWESOME...

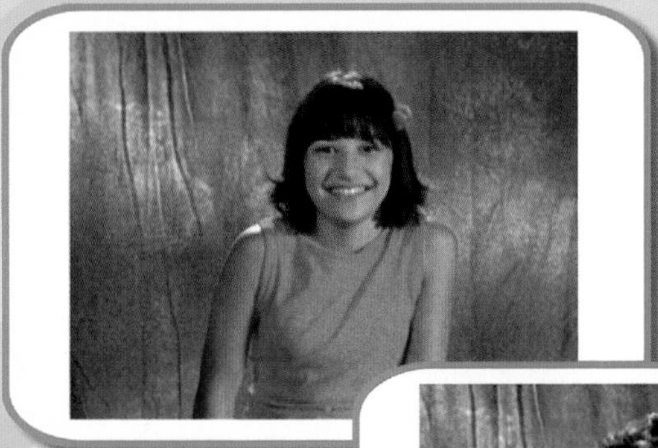

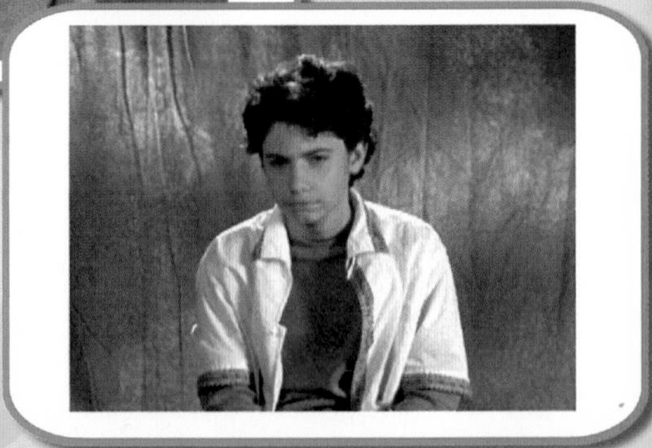

...AND GORDO LOOKED GREAT. ALL MOODY AND TROUBLED, LIKE FREDDIE PRINZE, JR.

Lizzie
McGuire

CINE-MANGA™ VOLUME 2

COMING SOON FROM TOKYOPOP®

BUT LIKE GORDO SAYS, I'D RATHER
BE A GOOD PERSON THAN LOOK
GOOD IN A PICTURE.

BESIDES, I LIKED THE WAY I LOOKED.

Well, she does
have the
sweater.

Still, I don't think
we need to order any
wallet sizes this year.

The End